Young at Heart

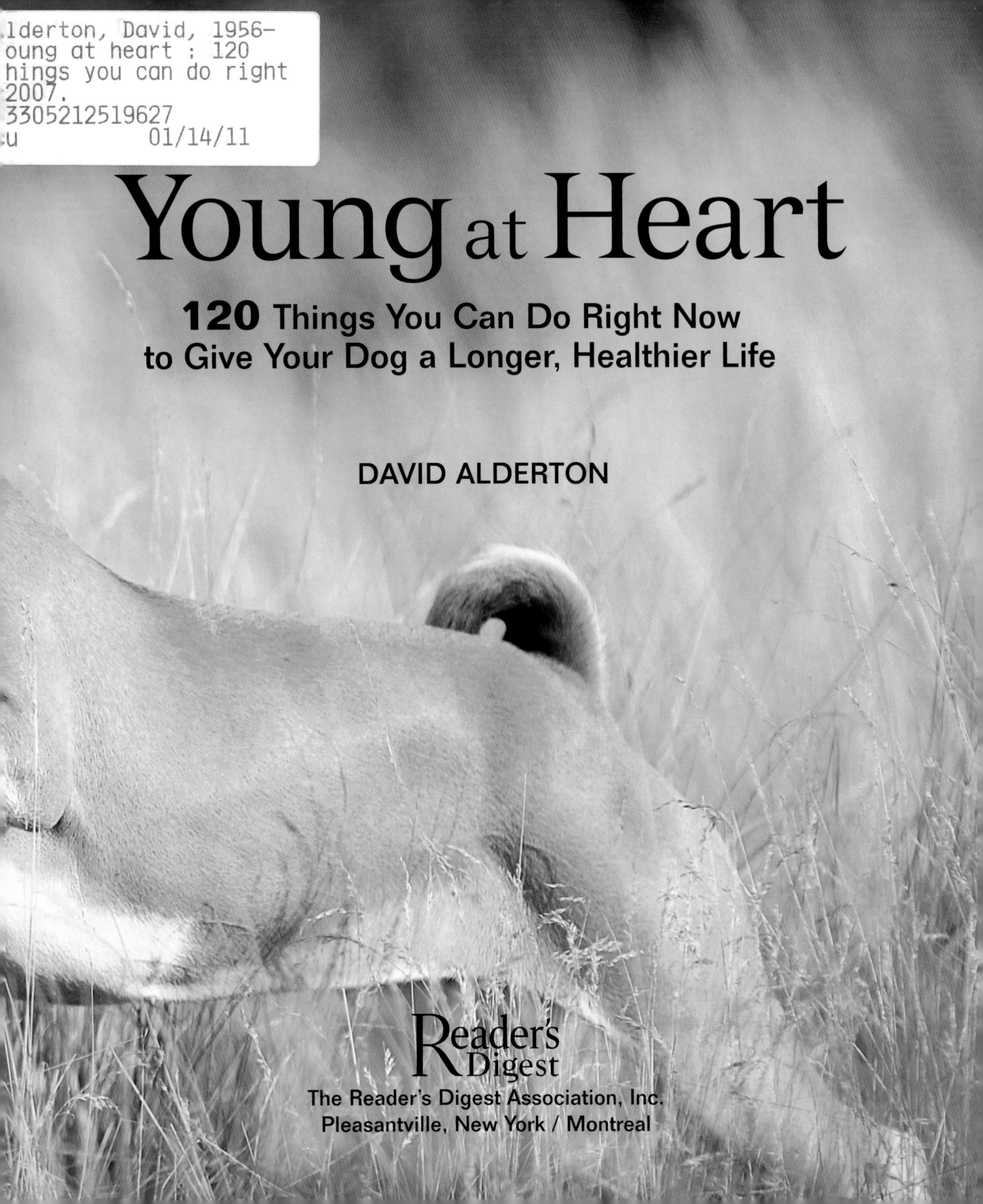

Young at Heart

120 Things You Can Do Right Now to Give Your Dog a Longer, Healthier Life

DAVID ALDERTON

Reader's Digest
The Reader's Digest Association, Inc.
Pleasantville, New York / Montreal

A Reader's Digest Book

This edition published by The Reader's Digest Association, Inc.
by arrangement with Toucan Books, Ltd.

FOR TOUCAN BOOKS

Design Bradbury and Williams
Editor Theresa Bebbington
Managing Editor Ellen Dupont
Index Michael Dent
Picture Research Christine Vincent
Proofreader Marion Dent
Front and back cover photographs
Dean MacLachlan

FOR READER'S DIGEST

U.S. Project Editor Kimberly Casey
Canadian Project Editor Pamela Johnson
Project Designer Jennifer Tokarski
Associate Art Director George McKeon
Executive Editor, Trade Publishing Dolores York
President & Publisher, Trade Publishing Harold Clarke

Library of Congress Cataloging-in-Publication Data:
Alderton, David, 1956-
    Young at heart: 120 things you can do right now to give your dog a longer, healthier
life / by David Alderton.
       p. cm.
    Includes index.
    ISBN-10: 0-7621-0679-4
    ISBN-13: 978-0-7621-0679-0
    1. Dogs. 2. Dogs--Health. I. Title

SF427.A545 2007
636.70893--dc22

                                                                           200604736

Address any comments about *Young at Heart* to:
The Reader's Digest Association, Inc.
Adult Trade Publishing
Reader's Digest Road
Pleasantville, NY 10570-7000

For more Reader's Digest products and information, visit our website at:
www.rd.com (in the United States)
www.readersdigest.ca (in Canada)

Printed in Singapore
1 3 5 7 9 10 8 6 4 2

NOTE TO OUR READERS
The advice given here should not be used as a substitute for that of a qualified veterinarian. No dogs or puppies were harmed
in the making of this book. In this book, unless the information given is specifically for female dogs, dogs are referred to
throughout as "he." The information is equally applicable to male and female dogs, unless otherwise specified.

Contents

Foreword

Within the last decade, the advancing knowledge of how dogs age combined with improved diagnostic technologies, newer medical therapies, and safer anesthetics allow today's veterinarians to better meet the medical and behavioral challenges of age-related problems in dogs more than ever before. These medical advances have been driven by the increased bonding between owners and their pets and by veterinarians' desire to provide improved care for their aging patients. In addition, commercial veterinary manufacturers have developed age-specific drugs, medications, and newer therapeutic diets focused on preventing or managing age-related problems.

Although it is impossible to turn back the hands of time, much can be done to cure, manage, or control common age-related problems. In addition to raising the standard of care for the older patient, veterinary health care is shifting from the traditional treating the sick patient to more proactive health maintenance and early detection strategies. Veterinarians are attempting to prevent age-related diseases with a combination of specially formulated senior diets, exercise programs, lifestyle changes, and routine checkups.

This book has a wealth of useful information to keep your pet healthy and young at heart. As a partner in the health care of your pet, it is my hope that as you read each chapter, you will educate yourself on the early warning signs of an impending problem. As a medical condition advances, the therapy options decrease accordingly. Therefore, favorable outcomes are often determined by an early diagnosis combined with timely intervention.

I would like to dedicate this book to my departed canine friends (Peekie, Shadow, Faith, and B. G.), who gave me firsthand education of the medical and behavioral problems associated with growing old.

William D. Fortney D.V.M.

Introduction

This book is in many ways a celebration, marking the way in which dogs are now living longer than ever before. Older dogs are forming an ever-increasing percentage of the canine population. As a result, a greater number of owners realize that these dogs have special requirements in their later stages in life—just as they did when they were puppies—to be sure they remain as healthy and active as possible.

An older dog can often enjoy a healthy life much longer due to medical advances and specialized diet foods.

The age at which a dog reaches the landmark of old age varies, depending on his size. While giant breeds may be considered senior at five or six years old, it is likely to be another couple of years before small dogs will reach the same point. However, in all cases, whether or not a dog is purebred, the steps that you take—particularly once your dog reaches middle age—will almost inevitably have a direct impact on your pet's overall life expectancy and the quality of his life.

How you should care for your dog is often based on common sense, much in the same way you should care for your own health. For example, avoid giving your dog unsuitable or too much food, which causes him to become overweight. Otherwise, excessive weight will place an increased and unwanted strain on your dog's body, and it often results in additional complications, such as diabetes. Apart from providing a second line of defense against weight gain, regular exercise is important in helping to keep your dog fit. Going out for regular walks will also help to provide your dog with mental stimulation, which is a vital aspect of countering the aging process for as long as possible.

Other less-obvious factors will also play an important role when it comes to ensuring the overall good health of a senior dog. A much greater understanding of the nutritional needs of a dog as he ages has led to the introduction of special foods that have been formulated to meet the particular requirements of an older dog. These senior diets can help to offset the most damaging effects of the aging process by addressing a dog's changing nutritional needs as he grows older. They will have fewer calories, for example, but also include other particular ingredients to offset the effects of the aging process.

Keeping your dog fit through exercise and a proper diet will help him stay healthy longer.

In cases where health problems may have already occurred, perhaps affecting one of your dog's organs, such as the heart or kidneys, there are also specialized prescription diet foods available from your veterinarian. These foods will help stabilize your dog's condition. Such foods are often used in association with regular medication, and together they can provide good results.

When things do go wrong, seeking prompt veterinary help will often ensure that even if a problem is not completely cured, your dog can continue to enjoy a reasonable quality of life. The great thing today is not just that dogs are living longer, but most significantly, they are remaining relatively fit and active well into old age.

In order for your dog to gain the most benefits as he grows older, you will need to combine all these different aspects together, taking account of your dog's individual needs to create what is effectively a lifestyle package. You can then be certain that you will be doing the best for your dog. And even if your dog's health falters as he ages, you should be able to concentrate on enjoying the extra years of company that you are likely to have with him as a result of today's medical improvements. In the past this would not have been possible in many cases.

CHAPTER 1

Bright-Eyed and Bushy Tailed

Not long ago, the typical life expectancy for a dog was less than a decade; however, a puppy born today will probably live well into his teens and could reach his early twenties. The oldest dog on record is Bluey, an Australian cattle dog that lived for 29 years. He worked for more than 20 years, which kept him physically and mentally fit.

A better understanding of the aging process has led to improvements in health care and greater nutritional knowledge. Owners have a vital part to play, too. By ensuring that your dog is fit and healthy in the early years of his life, he should encounter fewer health problems as he grows older.

What Is
Aging?

In general terms, the aging process is a battle between the body's genetic ability to renew itself and its ability to continue to function as it faces exterior challenges, such as diseases affecting its organs and difficulties in finding food.

In the wild, even hunters with few natural enemies, such as the gray wolf (*Canis lupus*)—the dog's ancestor—rarely reach the end of their natural life span. As the wolf's strength declines with age, its ability to hunt and obtain adequate food is reduced, too. This leaves the wolf at a greater risk of dying prematurely from disease, starvation, or both.

While it is not possible to affect the dog's genetically determined life span, having a better understanding of the aging process will make it possible to regulate the external factors that can have an impact and be controlled. This can help your dog

Puppyhood, according to kennel club definitions, lasts until the age of six months. Depending on the breed, juvenile dogs become adults when about one year old, with larger dogs maturing more slowly. Middle age is perceived as starting at about five years, with old age following around two years later.

Puppy: 3 months old

Adult: 4 years old

Elderly: 10 years old

to live to his maximum life span. In the past, many young dogs died early due to illnesses, such as distemper; however, now, thanks to the introduction of vaccines and their routine use, this cause of premature mortality is easily prevented.

The Stages of Aging

Just like humans, there are several stages to a dog's life span. Although puppyhood is a clearly defined stage, it is not always easy to determine when the other life-span stages—adulthood, middle age, and old age—begin and end. In general, once a medium-size dog reaches about 10 years old, he starts to slow down and is usually regarded as being elderly.

Of course, there are exceptions to the rules. Certain circumstances, probably the result of genetic factors, affect the aging process. The size of the dog is a significant factor. On average, large and giant breeds have a much shorter life expectancy than toy dogs, sometimes by several years. In addition, male dogs often have a slightly longer life expectancy than females of the same breed.

An Aging Canine Population

As the life expectancy for most dogs has increased, the number of older dogs in the overall canine population has grown, too. They now represent approximately 40 percent of the total figure, and half of these individuals are grouped in the elderly category. As a result, veterinarians are now much more familiar with the needs of older canine patients and how best to cater to them.

Comparing Dog and Human Years

Below is a guide to the equivalent number of dog years compared to human years, based on a dog's adult size. The green section represents the normal healthy adult years; the yellow, middle age, the years of slow decline in health; and the red, old age, when age-related diseases are of a chronic or serious life-ending nature. These are average figures—your dog may have a shorter or longer life span.

Adult Weight of Dog

	LB 0–20	21–50	51–120	120 PLUS
	KG (0–9)	(9.5–22.5)	(23–54.5)	(54.5 PLUS)
3 YEARS	28	29	31	39
4 YEARS	33	34	38	49
5 YEARS	38	39	45	59
6 YEARS	42	44	52	69
7 YEARS	46	49	59	79
8 YEARS	50	54	66	89
9 YEARS	54	59	73	99
10 YEARS	58	64	80	
11 YEARS	62	69	87	
12 YEARS	66	74	94	
13 YEARS	70	79		
14 YEARS	74	84		
15 YEARS	78	89		
16 YEARS	82	94		
17 YEARS	86			
18 YEARS	90			
19 YEARS	94			

Pet Age   Human Equivalent Age

When Your Dog Grows Older

Paws for thought...

A dog's senses often decline with age. His hearing will become less sensitive, and his eyesight may also deteriorate, with a milky opacity often developing in the eyes of an old dog. A dog with impaired eyesight or hearing will be less aware of dangerous situations. You'll need to be more alert to protect him from accidents or injury.

As your dog becomes older, his abilities and interests will change due to the effects of aging. By understanding aging, you can make adjustments to your pet's lifestyle to allow for these changes and to minimize their effects.

One of the most obvious signs that a dog is becoming older is a drop in his level of activity. Although dogs retain their desire to play until the end of their lives, your dog will probably slow down and not chase after a ball, for example, as enthusiastically as when he was a puppy. This loss of activity may not be noticeable, because many dogs still enjoy walking relatively long distances as they become older, even if they do not run as much. However, a dog suffering from hip problems, which are relatively common from middle age onward, may show signs of overexertion. These signs may only become evident later, such as your dog has stiff hind legs when he wakes up from a nap.

A reduction in activity may also be linked to weight gain. This often occurs with age, particularly in a neutered dog. Obesity worsens the symptoms of hip problems because the joints have to support more weight than usual. Try reducing your pet's food intake (see pages 52–53) to prevent obesity.

Great Danes and other giant breeds age faster than smaller dogs. At four years of age, Hugo is middle-aged, but he still plays tug-of-war with his owner.

Maintaining a level of regular activity, in the form of a daily walk or play session, is important not just for your pet's physical well-being but also to maintain his mental alertness. Most older dogs are happy to trot alongside their owners, although racing breeds, such as greyhounds, may still run fast when they feel in the mood.

Dietary Needs

If your dog has gum disease (see pages 28–31), he may find it painful to eat dry food. Dogs generally do not have problems with cavities in their teeth; however, erosion of the gum line can weaken the teeth at their roots, allowing infections to develop. This applies especially if there is a heavy buildup of tartar. It may be necessary to change from a dry food to a soft food because it is easier to eat.

The medical condition known as chronic kidney failure (see pages 94–97), which eventually affects most dogs in later life, will probably depress your pet's appetite and he will be more reluctant to eat. This is another reason to switch an older dog to canned food, which is generally more palatable than dry food.

Behavioral Changes

You'll notice a few changes in your dog's behavior as he ages. Older dogs like a set daily routine, so it is best not to change your dog's feeding time or make any other changes in his daily activities. An older dog often sleeps more, and when he wakes up, he may at first be confused about his surroundings. You may find that your dog is becoming more irritable, especially if his eyesight and hearing have been affected. In general, expect your older dog to prefer a more leisurely lifestyle than the energetic one he enjoyed as a puppy.

Resting after a run, these two Labs look happy.

Signs of Aging

Dogs age at different rates, and larger dogs usually show changes at an earlier stage than their smaller relatives.

Middle Age

- Still active but less boisterous than he was as a puppy.

- Starts to put on weight, particularly if he was neutered. Monitor his weight and cut back his food to avoid obesity.

- May consistently start to drink more water, an initial indicator of kidney failure.

Old Age

- Shows signs of stiffness and tends not to run as much as when he was younger; he needs less exercise.

- May become more fussy about his food because of dental problems or as the result of a more generalized illness.

- The coat of black dogs turns grayish around the muzzle.

- Likely to sleep more.

When to See
Your Vet

A Complete Checkup

Here are several of the most common procedures to expect at a dog's first "geriatric" screening:

- A record made of the dog's medical history, noting both his physical abilities and behavior.

- A complete physical examination: The vet will examine the eyes, ears, mouth, teeth, skin, and coat, and he will check the lymph nodes, abdomen, and the heart and lungs.

- Blood tests to check the complete blood count (CBC), which can detect certain problems, such as anemia, and to check the biochemical profile, which shows how the organs are functioning. Depending on where you live, a blood test may also be performed for heartworm.

- A urine sample to detect infections, diabetes, and kidney problems.

- A fecal examination to detect parasites.

Dogs are not only living longer, but just as significantly, they are now enjoying a better quality of life—thanks to the development of new treatments. It is important that you bring your dog to his veterinarian for regular checkups to make sure he will receive the best care.

By taking care of your dog's health, you are giving him the best chance of a longer, more comfortable life. Make sure that you are aware of the early indicators of an age-related health problem (see *Early Signs of Illness,* right)—and that you seek advice as soon as a potential problem arises. If your dog starts drinking more water, for example, it can be a symptom of several problems, including kidney failure and diabetes. Aside from the kidneys, other organs, such as the heart, function less efficiently as the years pass. Because regular veterinary checkups can detect such problems early on, your dog can receive medical assistance before serious complications arise.

Don't be worried about consulting your veterinarian. The symptoms of aging are not necessarily the beginning of the end. There is often a great deal that can be done at an early stage to stabilize a condition without affecting your dog's quality of life. Even if surgery is required— for example, to remove a tumor—the outlook is often much better if surgery is performed early on. The surgery will be less complicated, and the postoperative healing process should be quicker, too.

Regular Checkups

Your veterinarian should play an increasingly important role in the care of your dog as he becomes older, and this means more checkups, preferably twice a year. Many veterinarians are now offering an initial checkup for older dogs, sometimes referred to as a "geriatric" screening. It often takes place a few years before your dog reaches old age in an attempt to find and treat any problems as early as possible. When to have the first geriatric screening depends on your dog's size and when it is considered middle-aged (see page 13).

In addition to the procedures listed in *A Complete Checkup* (left), your veterinarian may perform other tests, depending on your dog and its history. If he finds a lump or small mass in the skin, for example, during the examination, a sample may be taken for medical tests. If a thyroid problem is suspected, then your veterinarian may want to do endocrine function tests. Chest X-rays or an abdominal ultrasound might also be required, and even an echocardiogram to check the heart.

Vaccinations

Even if you didn't keep all of your dog's vaccinations up-to-date beforehand, it is important to do so as your dog grows older. Vaccines and boosters are more important for an older dog because his immune system functions less effectively, making him more likely to succumb to infectious diseases. And depending on where you live, some vaccines, such as the rabies vaccine, are mandatory.

Discuss with your veterinarian which vaccinations and boosters are appropriate for your dog and how often. Among the ones to consider are those for distemper, hepatitis, leptospirosis, and parvovirus.

Taking your dog to a veterinarian is important not only when he needs treatment for an obvious condition or injury but also for regular checkups.

Early Signs of Illness

If you notice one or more of the following symptoms in your dog, it may be a sign of a problem. Be sure to bring your dog to a veterinarian for a checkup.

- Decreased appetite.
- Weight loss.
- Changes in behavior.
- Changes in activity levels.
- Less interaction with family members and other pets in the household.
- Episodes of confusion or disorientation.
- A change in sleeping patterns (sleeping too much or difficulty sleeping).
- Heightened thirst.
- Increased urination.
- Changes in housebreaking habits.
- More frequent bowel movements or constipation.
- Bad breath/red gums.
- Difficulty eating/chewing.
- Excessive panting or changes in breathing patterns/coughing.
- Collapse, fainting, or signs of weakness.
- Seizures.
- Tremors or shaking episodes.
- Difficulty climbing stairs or jumping up.
- Poor vision or hearing.
- New lumps or bumps.

Keeping Your Dog
Comfortable

As your dog becomes older, you'll need to adapt how you care for your dog to meet his changing needs. By doing so, you'll make your dog feel more comfortable.

Little things will mean a lot. Play with your dog every day and take him out for walks to provide both exercise and mental stimulus. Before taking your dog outside, check if it is cold or wet outside. If it is, protect your dog by providing him with a coat. An older dog is less likely to run, so he will feel the effects of the cold more quickly, especially if there is a high windchill factor. This applies particularly to a breed with a thin coat, such as a whippet, which gets cold more easily (see pages 32–33).

In warm weather, heatstroke (see page 33) is a possibility, so avoid exercising your dog around midday, when the temperature is the hottest. There is also another, longer-term danger linked to exercising an older dog in strong sunshine. It increases the risk of sunburn and developing skin cancer (see page 139), particularly if the dog is a pale color. The ears are especially prone to cancer. Try protecting them with a special canine sunblock.

Dietary Changes

Research and a better understanding of a dog's nutritional needs as it ages have revolutionized the dog-food market. Senior foods have been developed to ensure that the dog's body receives the necessary nutrients to function effectively (see pages 42–45). A diet consisting of senior foods can reduce the stress on the organs and help to combat the aging process.

A snap-fronted coat is easy to put on and comes off easily if it gets caught on something. This bright orange coat makes Milo, an eight-year-old Jack Russell, easy to find.

Your vet may recommend a specific diet as a preventative measure or to control a condition.

Comfort Around the Home

An older dog with stiff joints is less comfortable sleeping curled up in a traditional dog bed and will prefer to stretch out instead. A beanbag makes a great bed—there are various designs available for dogs in different sizes. Beanbags for dogs are more robust than those for people, and they have a washable outer cover, which you can strip off and wash so that the bed doesn't develop a doggy odor. Washing also controls fleas if necessary. Make sure your dog's bed is in a warm area (see page 33).

An older dog will usually have more difficulty in negotiating stairs and slippery floors. You may need to use safety gates to keep a dog away from potentially hazardous places. You may also require a ramp or steps to help a larger dog into a car (see pages 68–70).

Giving Your Dog Medicine

As your dog ages, it is more likely that you'll need to give him medicine, either short term or for the duration of his life. If you need to give your dog medicine, you can try disguising it in your dog's food (see *Giving Supplements*, page 27), but first discuss this with your veterinarian. For a serious condition, your veterinarian may want to ensure that your dog has his medicine by having you put it straight into his mouth.

To give your dog a pill or capsule, hold it between your thumb and index finger. Lift the upper jaw with your other hand, then lift the upper lip over the upper teeth to avoid being bitten. With the head held in a vertical position, and using the middle finger of the first hand near the small incisor teeth, open the lower jaw and slip the medicine onto the back of the tongue—it should fall to the back of the mouth. Close the jaws for a few moments, stroking your dog's throat or blowing gently on his nose to encourage him to swallow the pill.

10-Point Healthy Living Plan

1. Arrange a veterinary checkup for an older dog at least twice a year (see pages 16–17).

2. Adjust your dog's diet to an appropriate portion to prevent obesity. If your dog is overweight, help him lose weight (see pages 52–53).

3. Provide protection from the weather.

4. Play with your pet—mental alertness is important to his health (see pages 64–65).

5. Groom your dog regularly (see pages 34–35), and use this time to look for any swellings.

6. Provide your dog with regular daily exercise—avoid the occasional marathon hike, which could be more harmful than beneficial for your dog.

7. Keep your dog's vaccinations up-to-date.

8. Be sure that any medication is given regularly.

9. If you notice a change in your pet's behavior, seek veterinary advice.

10. Keep your dog away from situations in which a conflict can occur. Older dogs are at greater risk of being injured than younger ones.

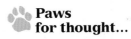 **Paws for thought...**

To give your dog a liquid medicine, use a needle-free syringe used for babies (available from pharmacies). While someone holds your dog, place the syringe into the side of his mouth, between his teeth, and gently apply pressure.

Choosing to Adopt a Pet

Paws for thought...

It can be much harder to cope with an older dog whose background is unknown or who has been mistreated. This type of dog is not a good choice for a home with young children. The dog could be more nervous and less tolerant than a dog that has grown up in a stable home environment.

An older dog from an animal shelter or rescue organization can be a wonderful pet. Shelters often have older dogs that need good homes.

Considering the competition from a cute puppy, it is understandable why it's more difficult to find a new home for an older dog. Yet there are benefits in choosing a mature dog. For example, he may have been the cherished pet of a person who could no longer care for him properly. An older dog from a loving home is often calmer; he should be well adapted to the domestic environment and less likely than a puppy to soil around the home or damage household objects.

Hopefully, a mature dog will also be well trained and more responsive than a young puppy, so he will be less likely to run away. Taking him out for a walk will be less of a problem once your new pet has bonded with you. This usually occurs within a few weeks, although the time span depends partly on how much time you can spend together. Initially, you will need to exercise your new pet on a leash until he becomes used to you.

Best friends belong together, which is why May and Jim were kept together when they were adopted.

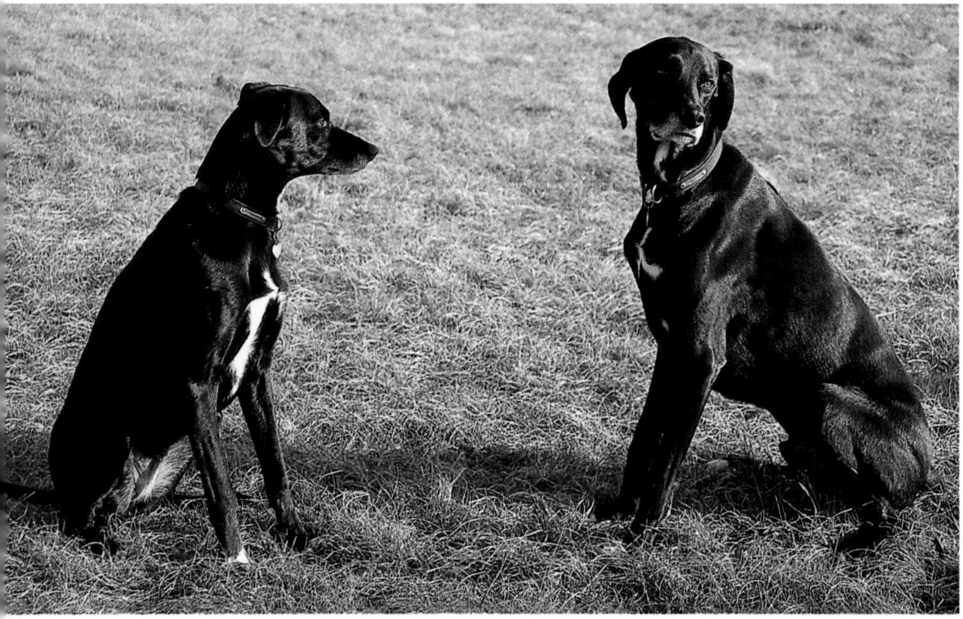

Adopting a Stray

When adopting a dog whose previous owner is known, you'll know how old the dog is. However, it's hard to know the age

of a stray dog. There are some general guidelines that you can use (see page 15) to determine if a dog is elderly, but these signs are less noticeable in a middle-aged individual. Large dogs often show more obvious signs of aging earlier in life than smaller dogs. It is difficult to work out the age of mongrels and crossbreeds of unknown ancestry.

Health-Care Costs

When thinking of providing a home to an older dog, many people worry that they will soon be facing large, ongoing veterinary bills. However, this is not necessarily the case, and taking out pet insurance can significantly offset unexpected costs. Make sure you compare a number of policies because some may offer benefits more applicable to your particular dog and situation. Beware of any exclusions, which may reduce the usefulness of the policy in the case of an older dog.

When an elderly dog has a preexisting medical condition, such as a heart problem, you may find that a rescue organization may be prepared to continue funding his treatment if you are able to offer a good home to the dog. This will free up kennel space so that the organization can help another homeless dog.

Introducing Your New Dog to Your Home

When you first arrive at home, be prepared to allow your dog to explore his new surroundings. Dogs depend on their sense of smell to orient themselves and investigate their environment. Your pet may be nervous at first, especially if you have recently had another dog in the home. In this situation, before your new pet arrives, thoroughly clean the carpets to eliminate the scent of the previous canine occupant. Otherwise, the newcomer may try to mask this scent by soiling areas around the home that your previous dog had marked—and you may confuse this behavior with an unwelcome lapse in housebreaking.

All dogs appreciate having a routine in their lives, and setting and sticking to a routine will help a newly adopted, older dog adjust to a lifestyle with you. It is not a good idea to change your new pet's name. A young puppy can usually get used to a new name, but it is much harder for an older dog to recognize a different name when he has already learned to respond to the sound of his existing name. He may simply not react if you use another name.

5 Steps to Adopting an Older Dog

1. Try to find out as much information as possible about your new dog in advance—both the good and bad!

2. When you acquire your new pet, make sure you arrange a veterinary checkup to learn about his state of health.

3. Be patient at first. You and your dog need to get to know each other.

4. Do not rush to let your new pet off the leash. He may not come back to you! Training classes may be a good idea if appropriate for your dog. You can teach an old dog new tricks.

5. Don't be afraid to ask for advice from your veterinarian if you need help. With an older dog, a problem may be medical. If not, your dog can be referred to a behaviorist.

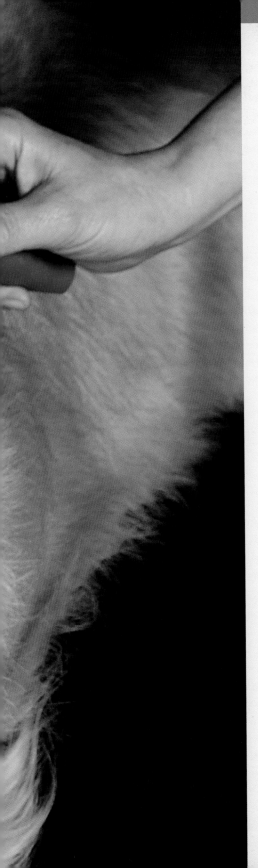

2 Taking Care of Your Best Friend

As a dog becomes older, his requirements will alter, reflecting the changes taking place in his body, so you'll need to modify the ways in which you care for your dog. For example, you'll have to take special care when grooming your dog and brushing his teeth.

It is important to be observant as you care for your dog. At close quarters you may detect swellings on the skin when grooming your pet, or you may notice that he is not eating in his normal manner. Watching your dog from a distance can also reveal symptoms, such as stiffness or persistent scratching. All these changes may indicate a problem that will need investigating by your veterinarian.

Why Older Dogs Need
Special Care

The changes that occur within a dog's body as he grows older affect all aspects of his life, including his appetite, level of activity, and physical abilities. This means that you will need to make corresponding adjustments to your pet's lifestyle as these signs of aging become apparent.

As a dog becomes older, he still needs physical activity, but he won't be able to do as much as he did in his puppy days. As a young dog, he may have easily jumped over a fence, for example, but as an older dog, he may struggle to reach the same height and hurt himself as he collides with the fence. If this happens, another effect of aging will become apparent: Injuries will be slower to heal.

With less exercise, the dog's muscles will lose strength and the dog will be more susceptible to the effects of cold weather. His mental abilities will also be affected by age, and your dog may be more forgetful. As your dog ages, it will become more difficult for him to perform his regular activities on his own, including grooming his fur.

Free Radicals and Aging

The actual changes affecting your dog's declining athletic and mental ability take place within individual cells in his body. During his life a dog is constantly exposed to chemicals derived from oxygen, known as free radicals. Although oxygen itself is vital for life, it can also have harmful effects in this form, accelerating the aging process. The free radicals combine with and damage cell walls, so cells function less effectively. Although some cells will replace themselves, such as those in the intestines, their ability to do so declines with age—and certain cells, such as those in the brain, cannot be replaced.

The free radicals can also interfere with the genetic material DNA, hampering the attempts of cells to regenerate in a healthy way. Interference to the body's DNA can trigger various diseases, notably the development of cancers.

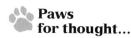

Paws for thought...

Your dog may not be aware that he is aging and will still continue to behave like a younger dog. This emphasizes the need for good training, because when you take your dog out for a walk off the leash, you may need to keep him close to you to prevent him from injuring himself.

A well-trained dog, such as this Labradoodle walking at heel, will respond to commands from his owner. This is useful in excitable situations where the dog may revert to puppy behavior.

Antioxidants to the Rescue

The body combats exposure to free radicals by utilizing antioxidants to counter the impact of these chemicals. Antioxidants consist of various enzymes produced in the body, along with vitamins and minerals from the diet. Unfortunately, as a dog grows older, his output of protective enzymes from the liver declines.

University studies have taken place to determine the impact of antioxidants on dogs. An initial study at the University of Toronto in Canada involved a group of beagles between 10 and 13 years old, and a second group between 3 and 5 years old. They were both fed a diet with antioxidants and mitochondrial enzymes, which are critical to the functioning of cells, with the aim of protecting against free-radical damage to the brain. Some of the dogs were also given tests to do each day to maintain their mental alertness, concentrating on skills that decline with age, such as a dog's ability to find his way back home by relying on landmarks. The diet had no effect on the young dogs, but those in the elderly group showed significant improvements in their mental faculties after only a month, especially among those that were being encouraged to use their mental faculties regularly.

The diet was also tried on household dogs of all types. Again, a noticeable increase in mental alertness was recorded, suggesting that the antioxidants were countering some of the effects of the aging process. This food has now become available commercially and can be prescribed by veterinarians for older dogs.

Common Antioxidants

Antioxidant enzymes are produced within the body, while nutrients, minerals, and trace elements are supplied in the diet.

Antioxidant Enzymes
Catalase; coenzyme Q10; glutathione peroxidase; superoxide dismutase (SOD)

Antioxidant Nutrients
Carotenoids and vitamin A; vitamin B complex; vitamin C; vitamin E

Minerals/Trace Elements
Copper, magnesium, manganese

The Role of
Supplements

Supplements have been traditionally used to ensure that a dog receives a balanced diet (see pages 42–45). However, there is growing evidence that a number of these chemicals also play a significant role in combating the aging process.

A senior dog may have greater needs for vitamins and minerals than his younger counterpart. As a dog becomes older, he loses his ability to absorb vitamins in the digestive tract, and if he has a kidney problem, for example, he may lose the B vitamins in his urine. However, high-quality commercial dog foods contain all of the vitamins and minerals that a dog will normally need, so if your dog's diet consists of one of these commerical foods, you will not need to give him supplements.

Antioxidants and Supplements

You can give your dog supplements of antioxidants (see page 25) to help delay the effects of aging. However, the way in which the individual antioxidant substances work differs; for example, lutein (a carotenoid) has an impact on the immune system. It ensures that the protective killer cells, which destroy harmful invading microbes, continue to replicate so there will be no decrease in their numbers with age, leaving the body at higher risk for infection.

If you give antioxidant supplements to your dog, do so carefully, preferably under veterinary advice. It is possible to overdose your dog with certain chemicals, such as vitamin A, which is stored in the liver. Too much vitamin A can have harmful effects on the body.

The Dietary Approach

There is an overall benefit of using a specially formulated diet with a combination of antioxidants instead of giving your dog individual components. The various components combined in a diet work on different parts of the system, creating a more effective synergy. Folic acid—a member of the vitamin B group—can assist in ensuring that

Natural Remedies

There are many natural supplements on the market, such as kelp (seaweed powder), a rich source of iodine that aids the functioning of the thyroid gland. To ensure there will be no adverse effects, seek your veterinarian's advice before giving a supplement to your dog.

the mitochondria, which are the powerhouses of cells, continue to function effectively, but by including specific fatty acids, which are a key component in the membranes around the cells, you can further improve cellular function. The membranes are where substances can freely enter and leave the cells, so an effective barrier is important. Other chemicals, such as carotenoids, are responsible for neutralizing the free radicals that can cause problems.

Supplements to Aid Mobility

Arthritis (see pages 114–15) is an area in which supplements have proved valuable. They can help to prevent damage to the cartilage lining the joints. In a healthy joint, the surfaces are lubricated and move smoothly so there is no pain; however, if damaged, the surfaces rub against each other, causing what can be severe discomfort.

Research has focused on New Zealand green-lipped mussels (Perna canaliculus). The mussels contain not only the compound glycosaminoglycan, which helps to protect the vulnerable matrix of the joint cartilage, but also certain omega-3 fatty acids, known as eicosatetraenoic acids (ETAs), which appear to protect against the pain of arthritis.

There are various supplements available on the market, so ask your veterinarian for advice about which to choose for your dog and the appropriate dosage. You can find supplements in health food stores, but not all are equally applicable for use with dogs. Glucosamine hydrochloride is preferred instead of chondroitin sulfate because tests have shown that it reaches a higher concentration in the joint. There has also been a move to incorporate these ingredients into some dog foods.

Giving Supplements

If you are giving your dog a powdered supplement, try to ensure that it is fed at least partially on wet food. The loose powder will not stick to dry food and will accumulate, uneaten, at the bottom of the food bowl.

Even if you are using capsules, it helps to use wet food. Try pressing a capsule into the food, concealing its presence from the dog. Most dogs bolt their food down quickly, so a capsule disguised in this fashion is often swallowed more easily than one given by hand. This is also true for medicines in pill form.

A licked-clean bowl is a good sign that Rowan, a 9-year-old collie cross-breed, has eaten all his food—supplements and all.

Maintenance for the
Mouth and Teeth

Some breeds are more prone to dental problems than others, with poodles being especially susceptible. By taking good care of your dog's mouth and teeth, you can prevent painful dental problems down the road.

Regular toothbrushing, accompanied by the occasional veterinary descaling if required, should make a significant difference to the state of your dog's teeth and gums, especially if combined with a healthy diet. The benefits will be particularly apparent when your dog is in his senior years. If you don't take care of your dog's teeth, he may need a number of his teeth extracted (see pages 98–99), which will make eating much more difficult as he ages.

Developing a Routine

Regular dental care involves brushing your dog's teeth about three times a week (although this should be daily if your dog has a gum problem). Brushing the teeth several times every week from an early age should help prevent a buildup of loose plaque, which leads to deposits of tartar forming. These mineralized deposits are hard and stick to the teeth. Thus, unlike plaque, they cannot be removed by brushing and will need to be removed by your veterinarian.

If tartar is left in place, the area of the gum in contact with it at the base of the tooth will soon become inflamed, causing the gum margin to recede, which will weaken the anchorage of the tooth in the jaw. There is also a further associated danger that bacteria will be able to gain access to the root of the tooth more easily, causing a painful abscess to form.

Brushing Your Dog's Teeth

There are special toothpastes and brushes available for cleaning a dog's teeth, and you should choose only these for your dog. Dogs often dislike the way in which ordinary toothpaste foams up, and they cannot spit it out of their mouths. In addition, ordinary toothpaste

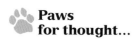
Paws for thought...

If your dog is reluctant to let you put your finger in his mouth, try dipping your finger in some beef bouillon and letting the dog lick it off your finger. Move on to rubbing your finger along the dog's gums, then use gauze flavored with the bouillon if necessary.

contains fluoride, which can be harmful to dogs, so it is important to use a toothpaste designed for a dog's teeth. The choice of toothbrush will depend on the size of your dog, how healthy his gums are, and how comfortable you are with brushing his teeth.

Although it is best to begin brushing a dog's teeth when he is a puppy, you can also start a toothbrushing routine in an older dog. Lift the dog's upper lip to brush his teeth. Start by gently rubbing gauze wrapped around your finger in a circular motion along the dog's teeth and gums to gain his trust. Then add toothpaste to the gauze before moving on to using a toothbrush. You will only need to brush the exterior surface of the teeth—the interior surfaces are cleaned naturally by the dog's tongue.

Benefits of Brushing
Good dental care early in life will pay dividends, simply because it should avoid the necessity of having to have your dog anesthetized for dental treatment by a veterinarian. Using anesthesia always has an unavoidable risk attached to it, particularly in the case of an older animal. However, this may be the only option to enable your veterinarian to clean your dog's teeth properly and to remove any teeth that have become loose or are diseased.

Crowded Teeth

Brachycephalic breeds of dog, such as the Boston terrier, are at greatest risk of having dental problems, because of the reduction in their jaw length, which is responsible for their shortened, rounded faces. Their teeth are more crowded and may even be distorted in the gum line, so particles of food can become more easily trapped between them, ultimately triggering the formation of plaque. If your dog is a breed of this type, pay particular attention to his oral hygiene.

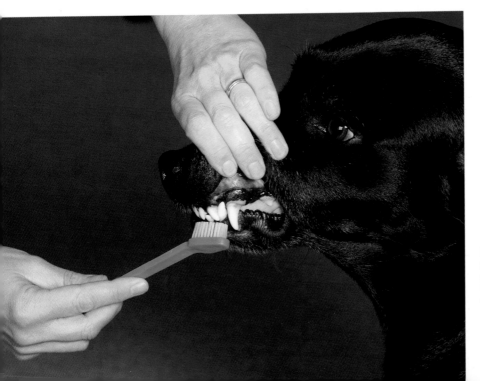

Practice makes perfect, and Jem's owner has had plenty of practice, having brushed the 8-year-old's teeth since she was a puppy.

Dental chews can help prevent plaque buildup. Some are treated with compounds that will help to freshen your dog's breath. However, if you suspect bad breath could be a symptom of kidney disease (see pages 94–97), arrange a veterinary checkup.

Dietary Prevention

Dry food has a slightly abrasive texture, so it helps to prevent a buildup of plaque on the teeth, which if left alone will be transformed into hard tartar and cause damage. There are also special dental chews now available that should help your pet's oral hygiene. Even an ordinary rawhide chew can be helpful, but try to prevent your dog from eating large chunks of this indigestible material, which can lead to intestinal problems.

Dog food manufacturers are now adding specific ingredients to dog foods in order to reduce the formation of plaque. These include sodium hexametaphosphate (often abbreviated simply to sodium HMP), which protects the teeth. Another approach involves the addition of polyphosphate crystals to block the actual mineralization of plaque into tartar on the teeth. Key features of this type are usually highlighted on the packaging of the food, and they will also be listed in the ingredients.

Dog Chews

The risk of tartar buildup is greater in older dogs that have a wet diet. Crunching dry food helps to keep the surfaces of the teeth cleaner, preventing plaque, and tartar, from developing.

If your dog eats wet food, offer him chews to help keep his teeth in good condition. Leather chews are better than bones to chew on, which can crack a dog's teeth and lead to digestive problems if broken-off pieces are swallowed. However, if you know that your dog's teeth are in poor condition, do not give him hard chews because they may cause further damage.

Doggy Breath

The long hair naturally present around the mouth in some breeds can be a source of bad odor from the mouth. It can easily become matted with food, particularly if your pet is fed fresh foods. You will need to groom this area carefully, washing it with a canine shampoo, and possibly trimming it back to prevent an immediate recurrence.

The scavenging habit that is natural for a dog often means that he will have an unpleasant array of bacteria within his mouth. Although it will not be possible to persuade your dog to use a mouthwash, you may need to apply a special gel incorporating a similar ingredient, such as chlorhexidine, to combact the bacteria. Your veterinarian may also recommend it to clean an area where a tooth has recently been removed to aid the healing process. Antibiotics are often prescribed as well, as a further precaution against the risk of an infection that began in the mouth from spreading elsewhere in the body.

As a preventive measure, you can buy toys impregnated with chlorhexidine or similar compounds, which should help to improve your dog's dental hygiene. There are also various commercially available items that claim to freshen a dog's breath, and you can also offer your pet fruit, such as sliced apple, for this purpose, too.

Even if you have recently acquired an older dog that has preexisting inflammation of the gums, offering your pet a dental chew should lead to an improvement in his condition within several weeks. These are specially designed to work away deposits of plaque on the teeth and therefore lessen any associated underlying inflammation.

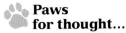

Paws for thought...

Check your dog's mouth periodically. Watch out for any unusual swollen areas, which could mark the start of a growth. Don't worry if the tongue is variable in color, with some dark areas—this is normal. A dark blue tongue is normal for the Chinese shar-pei and the chow chow.

Case History

Susie's Painful Gums

Susie is a 10-year-old border collie crossbreed that started rejecting her food. She ate it reluctantly and slowly—and then she tried to steal the cat's food. She started to lose weight, and her breath smelled bad. Fearing the worst, her owner took her to the veterinarian. After a thorough medical checkup, the cause of the problem turned out to be gum disease and two weakened teeth. They were making it painful for Susie to eat her dry food, but she could gulp down the softer cat food more easily. After dental treatment to clean the gums and remove the teeth (see pages 98–99)—along with a new regular toothbrushing routine—Susie began to eat her dry food again normally and put on weight—although she also continued to steal the cat's food if there was an opportunity!

The Importance of
Body Warmth

Dogs differ in the length and density of fur covering their bodies, a reflection of their area of origin and their need to keep warm. As a dog ages, his ability to keep warm diminishes, due to thinning hair and less activity.

Breeds from the cold far north are protected with a dense undercoat that traps warmth close to the body and a thick, weather-resistant top coat. At the other extreme are the so-called hairless breeds—the Chinese crested and the Mexican hairless dogs are the best-known examples. They are vulnerable to the cold. However, these dogs do possess a covering of hair, which is most evident on the extremities of their body, where heat is lost most rapidly from the body.

Heat Loss and Age

As dogs grow older, they feel the cold more partly because their body temperature becomes slightly lower as a result of a slowing down of their metabolism. This is often linked with a decline in the output of the chemical messengers known as hormones, which help to regulate the body's biological processes.

Physical changes in the structure of the body can also leave dogs more vulnerable to the cold. The muscles that enabled them to run quickly, generating heat as a result, decline in size with less use. Being less active means that an older dog will feel the cold, even shivering on occasions to raise his body temperature. With age, the hair covering the body may become sparser over certain parts of the body, lessening its insulating effect, while the skin—which also helps to retain heat—becomes thinner, too.

Keeping Your Dog Warm Outdoors

If you notice your dog becoming cold when outdoors, you can purchase a coat for him. You may need to buy at least two coats: a lightweight summer raincoat and a warm, waterproof winter coat if you live in an area with cold winters. You may want to try a sweater

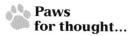 **Paws for thought...**

Although it is not safe to put a hot water bottle in a dog's bed, you can tuck beneath the bedding the type of heating pad often used to keep young puppies warm. These provide gentle warmth without any risk of burning the skin, and the electrical cord is protected in a metal casing, safe from the dog's teeth.

on a smaller dog to protect him from the cold, provided that you can put it on your dog without difficulty. However, there is a risk that your dog can become entangled if he ventures into undergrowth wearing a sweater. A regular coat is easier to wriggle out of should it get caught on branches or thorns.

You should take your dog to the store to ensure that the coat will fit properly before you purchase it. If you can't take your dog, many coats are sold as standard sizes for purebred dogs. For a mixed breed, you can assess the size of coat required by measuring the distance along your dog's back, from the neck to the base of the tail.

Warmth in the Home

Indoors, you will notice that your pet spends more time sleeping near a source of warmth, such as a radiator or an open fire. Make sure there is a secure guard around it to prevent any risk of the dog's coat from being singed. Keep your dog's bed in a warm position in the home, because the joints of an older dog that is cold can become stiff.

Hot Dogs

In hot weather an older dog, particularly one that has long hair, is at risk of heatstroke. A dog cannot cool his body by sweating in the same way as we do, because his sweat glands are confined to his paws. Instead, he pants so that the heat is dissipated from his body by the evaporation of water.

When the weather is hot, it is important to exercise your dog only in the early morning or during the evening—never at midday. This applies especially to a short-faced breed, such as a pug. He cannot cool his body effectively through his nose like a long-nosed breed and must resort to panting. The greater stress on a dog's weakened heart can be fatal.

Make sure you take a drink for your dog with you when you go outdoors. Never leave your dog in a car in hot conditions— this could be fatal.

Dogs with long fur, such as this 9-year-old Bernese mountain dog, have more difficulty coping with hot weather than cold weather.

Skin and
Coat Essentials

As a dog ages, the condition of his skin and coat changes. An older, less agile dog will need more assistance in grooming himself because he will find it more difficult to curl his head around to lick and nibble at his coat.

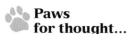

Paws for thought...

It is important to be aware of any warts or cysts, which commonly develop on the skin in older dogs. These are usually harmless, but a wart could be linked to cancer (see pages 138–43). Make sure you avoid disturbing warts when grooming your pet—they can bleed.

The hormonal changes that occur with age will affect an older dog's skin, which thickens and becomes less elastic, while the epidermis—the outer layer of skin—can become thin. At the same time, the production of the natural oils that protect the coat may decrease, leading to a dry, scaly coat. Because the changes are gradual, you may not notice the dog's coat losing its luster and becoming thin. Baldness, particularly over the flanks, may be due to a thyroid problem (see pages 128–33).

Grooming Your Dog

The amount of grooming that a dog requires depends not just on his age, of course, but also on his breed and coat type. A dog with a sleek, short coat, such as a greyhound, is easy to groom, needing little more than brushing with a hand glove or a rubber brush, which are available in pet stores. This brushing will act not only as a tonic for the skin—it stimulates the production of oil, which will help dogs with dry skin—but it will also give you the opportunity to check on the underlying condition of the dog's skin for any unexpected lumps or an

Regular grooming is necessary for dogs with medium-length fur, such as Rusty, an English toy spaniel, as well as for dogs with long fur.

increase in dandruff, which will need veterinary treatment.

In the case of a dog with longer hair, you will need to tease out any knots that develop in the coat before giving him a bath. You should work from the outer edges toward the center and avoid pulling the hair, which will be painful for your pet.

A slicker brush is traditionally used for long-haired dogs, but there are also combs available with rotating teeth that can be useful, too. Regular brushing will help prevent mats from developing. The areas most prone to mats are the backs of the legs, the front armpits, and behind the ears, so give those areas special attention.

Bathing

It is still important to bathe your dog regularly as he grows older, about once a month or so. This will maintain his coat and skin in good condition, but use a special canine shampoo for this purpose. Be prepared to lift your pet into the bath carefully (see page 69) to avoid aggravating any painful joints. Make sure you pay attention to areas that your dog may have difficulty in reaching, such as his hindquarters. It is also important to take particular care to ensure that your dog does not become cold afterward. Use a warm, large towel to dry your dog as thoroughly as possible.

Grooming Salon

In some cases, you may want to consider bringing your dog to a grooming salon. As well as long-haired breeds, other candidates include breeds with medium-length hair, such as an English toy spaniel, which can inadvertently stain their fur with urine or feces. This often occurs if there is a joint problem, which may cause a male dog to adopt an unusual position when urinating, or if your dog is suffering from constipation. You can ask for the overall coat to be trimmed back short, resembling the lamb clip often seen on poodles. This trimming will also have the advantage of making your pet more comfortable in hot weather.

> ### Calluses
>
> As giant breeds, such as Irish wolfhounds, become older, changes can occur at their elbow joints. The hair disappears and the underlying skin thickens, which can lead to the development of calluses. Although these calluses are a result of trauma, they do prevent abrasions from developing in a vulnerable area of the body, which could be injured when the dog rubs his elbows on the ground as he lies down.

Natural Remedies

If your dog's skin is dry and scaly, give him a fatty-acid supplement, such as fish oil.

A warm towel after a bath will help to dry your dog quickly and prevent him from becoming cold.

Caring for
Paws and Claws

A dog's paws play a crucial role in helping him to run or jump, as do his nails. It is important to care for the pads on the paws and to keep the nails trimmed to help your dog walk and run with the least amount of discomfort.

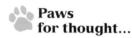

Paws for thought...

You should not try to use scissors when trimming your dog's claws—they are more likely to split the claw instead of cutting cleanly through the tissue as clippers do.

Guillotine-style clippers are the safest tool to use for trimming a dog's claws.

The claws help a dog to maintain his balance when running, and they are important for digging and grooming. Some breeds, such as Newfoundlands, have webbing between the toes to help them swim. The bottom of the paws is protected with pads. Although these may appear dry and horny, they bleed profusely if cut.

The pads thicken with age, but this is not a problem. However, older dogs exercise less often, so they are susceptible to overgrown claws. The claws do not wear down to the same extent as those on a younger dog, so they become longer than normal, growing away from the paws. If left alone, the overgrown claws can lead to a handicap, particularly in small dogs, such as Yorkshire terriers.

Trimming the Claws

Although you can ask your veterinarian or dog-grooming salon to trim your dog's claws, you can do it yourself if you invest in a stout

End of living tissue

pair of clippers. Suitable guillotine-type clippers with scissorlike blades are widely available from pet stores and are easy to use.

A dog's claws have a central inner, living core, which has nerves and receives a blood supply. At their tips the tissue is dead—the same as our own fingernails. You can usually see a pink area where the living tissue ends on most breeds, which aids in trimming the claws. However, in breeds that have black claws the pink area is not visible, so you'll need to be more cautious when cutting the claws. If you cut the claw back too short, it will start bleeding. It is important to have someone else restraining your dog so you can hold the paw and concentrate on cutting the claw properly.

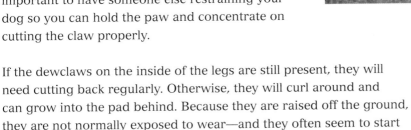

After every walk through a field, Bernie's owner inspects his feet for seeds lodged between his toes.

If the dewclaws on the inside of the legs are still present, they will need cutting back regularly. Otherwise, they will curl around and can grow into the pad behind. Because they are raised off the ground, they are not normally exposed to wear—and they often seem to start growing more prominently in older dogs.

Painful Walks

After a walk through fields, especially in hot, dry weather, it is important to check your dog's feet for grass seeds that may become lodged in the fur between the toes. Burrs and similar sticky seeds may be found higher up on the leg or the body itself, but they tend to be much more conspicuous and are easily removed. The effect of a grass seed between the toes is often severe and can cause your dog serious distress.

The sharp ends of many grass seeds allow them to penetrate the skin, like a splinter, and a lodged seed may ultimately cause an abscess if left in place. Your dog will nibble repeatedly in the area of irritation but will often be unable to remove the seed. If you want to examine the area yourself, take particular care and have someone else restrain your pet, because the pain can be so intense that the dog may bite when you touch the affected area. It is better to seek veterinary advice so the seed can be removed while the dog is under sedation.

Natural Alternatives

When trimming your dog's claws, have some flour at hand. If you accidentally cut too close to the quick and the claw bleeds, apply the flour to the claw to help stop the bleeding.

Flea Control and
Deworming

Dogs are vulnerable to fleas and worms throughout their lives; however, modern methods of controlling these parasites mean that they should not be an insurmountable problem—except in cases of repeated exposure.

An older dog who has been repeatedly bitten by fleas earlier in life can develop a fleabite allergy. In this case, just a single bite from a flea can trigger what can become a widespread allergic reaction to the flea's saliva, which is injected by his mouthparts into the skin when he feeds. The dog will start to scratch with a greater intensity than occurs with a simple fleabite, and he will nibble ferociously at his skin. At first, raised red pimples will be seen on the dog's skin, most obviously on the underparts where the fur is thinner, and the skin may subsequently alter in appearance, becoming darker.

If your dog has fleas, ask your veterinarian to recommend the most suitable product for treating your dog.

To determine whether your dog has fleas, you will need a special fine-toothed flea comb. Use this on your dog outdoors—if any fleas leap off and escape, they

The Flea's Life Cycle

The female flea produces tiny white eggs, which drop off into the flea's surroundings, especially a dog's bedding. These will hatch into larvae within approximately 12 days. Subsequently, the larvae pupate after two weeks, and they ultimately emerge from their cocoons when triggered to break out by such indicators as an increase in temperature or movement nearby.

won't infest your house. Concentrate on the dog's back, especially the area just in front of the base of his tail, because this is where fleas congregate most often.

Even if you do not see any adult fleas, watch out for specks of black dirt, which turn reddish if dropped onto a wet piece of paper towel. This is flea dirt, which contains the undigested remains of your dog's blood. It indicates that your dog has fleas—or if there are none present, that they had been and might have left behind eggs.

Combating Fleas

It is absolutely vital to completely eliminate the fleas from the dog's environment to prevent reinfection, as well as to treat your pet. Fleas spend only a relatively small proportion of their lives on a dog, and for every one that you find, there can be 100 more fleas in various stages of development nearby. A cat or another dog sharing the home may also be infected.

You will need to treat your dog with a suitable insecticidal product that kills adult fleas, instead of one of the insect-growth regulators or similar products that block the completion of the flea's life cycle. In addition, strip down the dog's bed, wash it thoroughly, and vacuum the surrounding area, cleaning as close to the walls as possible because this is where larvae often lurk. Spray the area with a safe insecticide (but be particularly careful if you have an aquarium, because such compounds are often deadly to fish). Do not forget to treat other areas where your dog spends time and could have left flea eggs, such as on the upholstery in the room or in a car.

The Heat-Lover Hookworm

Although tapeworms are unlikely to be fatal, some other parasites, such as hookworms, can kill an older dog. Hookworms occur in warmer parts of the world, including the southern parts of the United States and in Australia. It is virtually impossible to prevent exposure to hookworms, because they occur in wildlife, and the larvae can enter the dog's body between its toes, after being picked up from the ground. For a dog living where these worms occur, regular deworming is essential.

Parasitic Worms

Fleas can mean the presence of another hazard: The tapeworm *Dipylidium caninum,* which develops in the dog's intestinal tract if your dog inadvertently catches and swallows a flea while grooming himself. Although the greatest focus on deworming treatment is on puppies, it is also important for older dogs. In fact, puppies may acquire roundworms from their mother prior to birth. To prevent this transmission, it is important that you worm adult dogs twice yearly.

CHAPTER 3 Adapting Your Dog's Diet

Dogs love to eat, and they will often consume more than is good for them if allowed. A natural scavenging instinct, in which a dog gorges on food whenever it is available, is responsible for this behavior. Even if you are careful about the amount of treats you give your dog, the composition of most modern diets can make it easy to overfeed him. Providing just a little in excess of the recommended amount on a daily basis will soon lead to your dog becoming overweight. Make sure you follow the instructions for using all canine foods carefully, particularly when changing from one brand to another, because they usually differ.

Giving Your Dog the
Right Foods

Caution

Do not confuse senior diets with prescription diets. The latter are available only from a veterinarian, and they have been formulated to address specific health problems often associated with older dogs, such as chronic kidney failure.

A home-prepared diet can include tomatoes, an excellent source of vitamin C.

All dogs need a diet balanced with the appropriate amounts of carbohydrates, protein, fats, vitamins, and minerals. These nutritional ingredients are exactly the same in senior dog foods as those found in standard foods; however, their proportions differ, especially if your veterinarian has prescribed a special diet food for a health problem.

For an older dog, choose a high-quality dog food made by a reputable manufacturer. These premium foods are designed for the nutritional needs of a senior dog. They often are lower in protein, sodium, and phosphorus, while they may be higher in certain vitamins. In general, a dry food is a more concentrated source of nourishment than a canned food, so if you need to help keep your dog's weight under control, a dry food might be a better choice.

The Components in a Senior Diet Food

A dog derives most of his energy from carbohydrates, which are found in plants such as rice and wheat. Older dogs are less active, so the carbohydrate level in a senior diet is reduced, because any excess carbohydrate will be stored in the body as fat.

Certain fats, known as essential fatty acids (EFAs), are also vital components of the diet; however, they cannot be manufactured in the dog's body. A deficiency often shows up as a dry coat full of dandruff. EFAs can also have an impact on the immune system.

Proteins, which are important to aid a young dog's growth, are needed in an older dog to help the healing process. However, the emphasis in senior diets is on easy digestibility, so the amount of protein in the food is usually reduced slightly to make it easier for an older dog to digest. There may also be extra fiber to guard against constipation.

Vitamins and minerals (see pages 44–45) are also essential dietary components, fulfilling a range of functions in the body. These include playing a key role in metabolic processes, as well as helping to combat infections. In a senior diet the level of phosphorus may be reduced, for example, to take into account the inevitable decline in kidney function that occurs with age, even if the dog does not have symptoms of kidney failure.

Nutraceuticals, such as antioxidants, chrondroitin, and glucosamine, which are substances believed to have therapeutic benefits, are often included in a senior diet to counter symptoms of aging. Because these foods are nutritionally complete, you will not need to supply your dog with a vitamin and mineral supplement.

> ### Senior Foods
>
> Foods that are specifically made for older dogs will meet the dogs' changing nutritional needs. They are usually recommended for dogs over seven years old, depending on the breed, and include:
>
> - A lower level of more easily digested protein to protect the kidneys.
> - Fewer calories, reflecting the lower energy requirement of older dogs.
> - Higher levels of essential fatty acids to keep the coat in good condition.
> - Increased vitamin levels—these help protect important body functions and offset the aging process.
> - More fiber to offset the increased risk of constipation.
> - Joint supplements, such as glucosamine, to aid mobility, especially if a dog has arthritis.

Home-Prepared Dog Food

If you have always fed your dog home-prepared food instead of commercially formulated foods, altering his diet to take into account his changing nutritional needs will be more difficult. You can cut back on carbohydrates easily, but seek veterinary advice before adjusting the vitamin and mineral requirements.

Changing Your Dog's Diet

The stage at which to switch your dog from a standard diet to a senior diet will depend on your particular dog and his individual state of health. As a preventative measure, it may be worthwhile to take advantage of the benefits that these foods should bring. When changing your dog's diet from one food to another, it is advisable to do so over the course of a week or so. This will lessen the likelihood of any associated digestive upset that can occur as your dog gets used to the new components provided in his new food.

The occasional treat will do no harm. But don't give your dog too many—as he grows older, the additional calories will cause him to gain weight.

Shiny fur is one indication that 8-year-old Mollie is enjoying a healthy, well-balanced diet.

Fat-Soluble Vitamins

These are stored in the dog's liver, so excessive dosages over a period of time can build up and have toxic effects.

Vitamin A Found in cod liver oil, eggs, and milk. A precursor form in plants, known as carotenoids, can be converted to active vitamin A in the dog's body—carrots are a good source. Vitamin A is needed for healthy eyesight and by certain membrane structures in the body.

Vitamin D Sunlight is a natural source of vitamin D. This vitamin is responsible for maintaining a healthy skeleton—it adjusts and controls calcium and phosphorus levels, including their absorption from the intestinal tract.

Vitamin E Wheat germ is a source for vitamin E, which keeps a dog's skin healthy and provides cardiovascular benefits. Vitamin E also works with the mineral selenium as an antioxidant, combating free radicals.

Vitamin K Produced naturally by bacteria that naturally occur in the dog's intestinal tract, vitamin K plays an essential role in the blood-clotting process.

Water-Soluble Vitamins

These are lost from the dog's body through urination. A deficiency can occur if a dog has chronic kidney failure.

Vitamin B Complex A range of compounds that are vital to the body's metabolism are known as vitamin B complex. They include thiamine (B_1), riboflavin (B_2), pyridoxine (B_6), pantothenic acid, niacin, and biotin (sometimes called vitamin H). It is easy to compensate for a deficiency with one of the supplements of yeast-based products formulated for dogs as a source of the B vitamins.

Vitamin C Another vitamin produced in the dog's body—in the liver in this case—is vitamin C. It serves as a natural antioxidant (see pages 26–27). Unless your dog is not able to manufacture this vitamin, supplements are not normally advisable. A deficiency of vitamin C causes scurvy, which results in sore, bleeding skin.

Minerals

Minerals sometimes react with each other, so keeping these elements balanced in a diet is important for your dog.

Calcium and Phosphorus A correct balance of calcium and phosphorus is vital to ensure a healthy skeleton. A diet based on meat alone will be harmful because meat is an insufficient source of calcium. There is also a risk of a calcium deficiency if your dog has chronic kidney failure. This is because calcium is lost through urination, while phosphorus builds up in the blood. Calcium may be removed from the skeleton to counter the high level of phosphorus. Your veterinarian will recommend a supplement or suggest switching your dog to a chronic kidney prescription diet.

Other Minerals Along with calcium, sodium and potassium are needed for nerve impulses and muscular contractions. Excessive amounts of sodium are believed to be a factor in raised blood pressure (hypertension). Impaired kidney function may have an impact on the levels of these minerals. Magnesium is essential for healthy nerve and muscle tissue and function. Iodine is a vital component of the hormones produced by the thyroid glands to regulate the body's metabolism. A deficiency in zinc can sometimes be linked with a vegetarian diet. Zinc has a number of different key roles in the body, but especially in ensuring a healthy coat. It also helps the functioning of the immune system. Selenium is another key element for a healthy immune system, combating free radicals (see pages 24–25). It can be toxic in excess, and supplements are not recommended. Copper and iron are utilized by blood cells. These minerals are linked with the transport of oxygen and carbon dioxide.

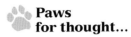

Paws for thought…

All general dog foods have similar ingredients, but their main meat constituent varies. Dogs are not normally fussy about their food unless they are ill, so it doesn't matter which brand you choose unless your pet has a food allergy. Hypoallergenic diets contain meat, such as venison and duck, that usually do not trigger an allergic reaction (see pages 54–55).

Just a little sunshine provides these two lifelong friends with plenty of vitamin D.

Food and the
Older Dog

As your dog becomes older, it will become increasingly important to regulate his daily food intake. Your dog's level of activity will generally decline from middle age onward—and if the dog's food intake remains the same, he will start putting on weight.

Unfortunately, weight gain in dogs can be insidious, particularly in the case of breeds with a thick coat, and unless you do regular checkups on your dog's weight (see page 50)—about once a month—you may soon have an obese pet before you are aware of it. If your dog has a health condition, such as a kidney problem, you may also need to keep a close watch on your dog's diet and his weight (if he loses weight, it may be an indicator that the problem is becoming worse). In such cases, and where a dog needs to lose weight, monitor your dog's weight on a weekly basis.

Breed Differences

Certain breeds, such as basset hounds and Labrador retrievers, are particularly susceptible to putting on weight. However, not all breeds are gluttons, and some dogs, such as greyhounds and whippets, display less of a tendency to put on weight as they grow older. It will soon become apparent if a dog in the latter category is gaining weight because his conspicuously sleek, athletic outline will start to disappear. His natural instinct to run also helps him to stay fit and burn off calories. A greyhound or whippet will continue to run regularly right to the end of his life—although not at the same pace as when he was younger.

Lack of Appetite

Although a slim dog will probably be healthier than one that is obese, it is equally important to be alert to any loss of appetite or weight because this is often a sign of ill health. Even if your dog has always displayed a tendency to be fussy about his food, which is often the case for toy breeds, such as Chihuahuas, it is still important to have

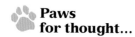
Paws for thought...

Neutering your pet can lead to weight gain. In most cases, reducing a neutered dog's food intake by 20 percent should help to keep his weight stable.

your pet checked by your veterinarian in case there is an underlying health issue, such as chronic kidney disease (see pages 94–97), or a dental problem that can make eating painful (see pages 28–31).

Fussy About Food

You can increase the palatability of a dry diet by allowing the required quantity to soak in a little warm water for a few minutes before feeding your dog. This will soften the food's texture and create gravy, too. However, any food left uneaten should be discarded—it will start to turn moldy soon after becoming wet.

If your older dog is simply disinclined to eat, you can usually rekindle his appetite by changing his diet. For a dog that has been fed on dry dog food beforehand, you can try switching him to a canned product—it will probably be much more tasty, and if your dog has lost a number of its teeth, it will be easier to eat.

A dog's sense of taste and smell will decline as he becomes elderly, which makes food less appealing. If you feed your dog fresh food, try warming the food, either directly or by pouring some gravy over it. Special low-salt (sodium) products are available specifically for dogs; alternatively, you can make your own easily from a meat stock.

Dogs that pile on weight include the basset hound, one of the more susceptible breeds— however, with your help, your dog can escape this outcome.

Top 10 Overweight Breeds

Some breeds are more prone to developing obesity. If your dog belongs to one of the breeds listed below, it doesn't mean that he will become obese. However, you should be diligent in helping him to maintain a healthy weight. Here are the top 10 breeds most susceptible to obesity and their ideal weights.

Breed	Weight
Basset hound	40–60 lb. (18–27kg)
Beagle	18–30 lb. (8–14kg)
Bulldog	50–55 lb. (23–25kg)
Cairn terrier	13–16 lb. (6–7.5kg)
Cavalier King Charles spaniel	10–18 lb. (5–8kg)
Cocker spaniel	24–28 lb. (11–13kg)
Dachshund (miniature)	9–10 lb. (4–4.5kg)
Golden retriever	60–80 lb. (27–36kg)
Labrador retriever	55–75 lb. (25–34kg)
Norwegian elkhound	44–50 lb. (20–23kg)

Is Your Dog
Overweight?

A dog that remains near his optimal weight throughout life will probably live longer and enjoy a better quality of life than a similar dog that is obese. Obesity often causes, in effect, premature aging, simply because the dog no longer retains the stamina or physical ability to play as he did in the past.

It is no coincidence that working dogs, such as sheepdogs, often have a longer life span than other dogs. Although their lifestyle may leave them more vulnerable to joint ailments, their overall level of fitness makes them less likely to develop medical problems that are associated with a sedentary existence and that can curb their life expectancy. Working also demands mental alertness, which helps to delay any impairment of mental function. By making sure your own dog maintains his ideal body weight, you will be helping him to have a happier, longer life.

Determining Your Dog's Ideal Weight

Monitoring your dog's weight (see page 50) is a critical part of dog ownership, and this will become more important as your dog ages. It can help you to determine if there is a sudden change in your dog's weight, which can be a symptom of an underlying health problem, such as chronic kidney failure (see pages 94–97).

In the case of a purebred dog, his ideal weight is typically indicated by the breed standard, which specifies the dog's distinguishing characteristics, so you can use your bathroom scales to establish if your dog's weight is okay. However, if you own a crossbred or mongrel—instead of a bathroom scale— you will need to rely on your observations to assess the dog's body condition, which will help you to determine if the dog's weight is okay.

A slim dog, such as 11-year-old vizsla Ziggy, will stay healthy and active longer than a dog that is overweight.

Body Condition Examination

The first step to determine if your dog's body condition is okay is to examine his ribs. Run your hands down over his rib cage. You should just be able to feel these bones, which protect the chest cavity. This should be possible even in the case of a dog with a long coat. There are other signs that are also important in determining your dog's body condition (see *Is Your Dog's Weight Okay?*, right). For example, the hip bones should be evident on each side of the tail and you should be able to see an abdominal tuck—the area behind the ribs that should be smaller in diameter than the chest. (*Note:* The amount of abdominal tuck varies between breeds.)

If the hip bones appear to protrude too much and the dog has prominent ribs, these indicate that your dog is underweight. If your pet has been eating normally, this is a sign that there could be an underlying health problem that will need veterinary investigation. Conversely, if you cannot feel the ribs and your dog has other signs of being overweight, you will need to take action to help your pet to lose weight (see pages 52–53).

Belly Alarm

A taut belly is another sign of good body condition in a dog. This area of the body should definitely not droop down and feel flabby, because this indicates a buildup of unwanted fatty tissue. External signs of obesity are possible indicators of a more sinister change that may be taking place internally in an obese dog. Abnormal deposits of fat can build up around body organs, such as the heart, and may also infiltrate the liver, compromising the efficiency of these organs.

Is Your Dog's Weight Okay?

By observing and feeling for these conditions, you can determine if your dog's weight is okay.

Underweight

- The ribs, spine, shoulders, and hip bones can be seen from a distance.

- You cannot feel or see any body fat.

- You see a prominent waistline when looking at the dog from above.

- Looking at the dog from the side, the abdominal tuck is too extreme.

Ideal weight

- You can feel the ribs easily, along with a slight amount of fat over them, with each rib being distinct. The spine, shoulders, and hips can be felt under a small amount of fat.

- A slight covering of fat, which should feel smooth, covers the area by the base of the tail.

- Looking at your dog from above, you can see that there is a definite waistline.

- Looking at your dog from the side, there is a modest abdominal tuck.

Overweight

- You cannot feel the ribs or the bones at the spine, shoulders, and hip because there is too much fat.

- You cannot feel any bones beneath the covering of fat near the base of the tail.

- Looking at your dog from above, there is no waist—or where it should be, the area is wider than the ribs and hips.

- Looking at your dog from the side, there is no abdominal tuck.

Your Dog and
Obesity

An obese dog is defined as one that exceeds his ideal weight by more than 15 percent. Being obese will reduce a dog's quality of life at any age. However, in the case of an older dog, obesity is a serious and potentially life-threatening condition.

The origin of obesity can often be traced back to puppyhood, and research has revealed that fat puppies will probably grow into obese dogs. Excessive weight gain restricts the mobility of a dog, making him less capable of running and exercising. This marks the start of a downward spiral, because unless the dog's food intake is reduced, his weight will continue to increase, which only worsens the problem.

A Strain on the Joints

Being heavier than normal puts additional strains and stresses on the body's musculoskeletal system. In fact, one of the most common injuries experienced by obese dogs is a ruptured cruciate ligament, which normally helps to stabilize the knee (stifle) joints. The injury will cause both pain and lameness, and your dog may need surgery to repair it. The most important step to take to minimize the risk of recurrence will be to place your dog on a diet so that he loses weight.

Arthritis (see pages 114–15) is usually both more common and more severe in obese dogs. It can deter your dog from walking, which will make it harder to address and correct the underlying problem of your pet's weight.

Obesity and Your Dog's Heart

Internally, having to carry extra weight around will probably place the heart under additional strain, and in older dogs this organ will not function as effectively as in a younger individual. This increases

Weighing Your Dog

You can't tell all dogs are at their correct weight by weighing; however, weighing a dog on a monthly basis will alert you to a possible problem if your dog begins to either lose or gain weight. If your dog is on a weight-loss program, you'll need to monitor his weight every week.

You can weigh your dog using your own bathroom scale. For a smaller dog, stand on the scale while holding your pet, and then subtract your weight from the total—this result is your dog's weight. For a larger dog, try persuading your pet to sit on the scale so you can weigh him directly. If your dog needs to lose weight, keep a record of the results and monitor his progress on a weekly basis.

the risk of heart failure and high blood pressure (hypertension). Furthermore, if the heart is working less efficiently, it can have widespread effects on other parts of the dog's body because of its key role in the circulatory system. Less oxygen will be carried by the red blood cells to the brain, which can affect the cells in the brain and contribute to a loss of mental faculties. The lungs are also affected because too much fat restricts the area in which they can expand— another factor that will decrease the amount of oxygen reaching the cells around the body. Obesity also has an impact at cellular level elsewhere, and obese dogs are more vulnerable to diabetes mellitus (see pages 134–37) and cancer (see pages 138–43), too.

Skin and Coat Problems

An overweight dog will have more folds of skin, which may form pockets where bacteria can thrive and infections can develop. This applies particularly to certain breeds that have natural folds of skin on their bodies, such as the Chinese shar-pei or the bloodhound.

In hot weather your dog will probably experience more discomfort than usual if he is overweight, and you may need to lessen his distress by acquiring a fan or supplying a portable air-conditioning unit to keep him cool. Do not forget to ensure that, as usual, he also has free access to drinking water.

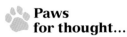

Paws for thought...

If your dog weighs too much, pay attention to where he lies down. Because of his weight, he can develop pressure sores on his underside. For example, encourage the dog to lie on a soft surface instead of tiles— even if these are cooler and more comfortable in hot weather.

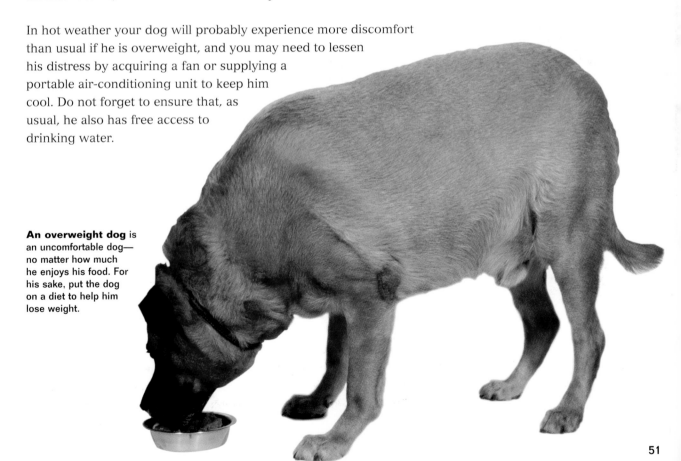

An overweight dog is an uncomfortable dog— no matter how much he enjoys his food. For his sake, put the dog on a diet to help him lose weight.

Helping Your Dog
Lose Weight

If you need to help your dog lose weight, make sure you enlist the involvement of the entire family—there is no point in attempting to enforce a weight-reduction program if other members of the family slip tidbits to the dog without your knowledge.

Even if your dog is overweight, never be tempted to put him on a crash diet, because this can cause severe metabolic disturbances, particularly in an older dog. You may also find that your dog will react by seeking to steal food at every opportunity, whether in the home or when you are out for a walk. Instead, devise a realistic weight-loss plan for your pet with the help of your veterinarian.

Many veterinary clinics now operate weight-loss clinics for pets, where you can obtain ongoing advice about your pet's progress and his diet, along with an accompanying exercise program to help your dog burn off the unwanted calories. You'll need to monitor the effects of the diet by weighing your dog (see *Weighing Your Dog,* page 50) once a week.

Diet Food for the Dog

A prescription diet food is the easiest way of feeding a dog on a weight-loss program. It contains a balanced range of ingredients and requires no other additives. Virtually all dogs can be switched to this type of food without experiencing any difficulties. Over the course of about one week, gradually increase the volume of the new food and decrease the volume of the old food until you're feeding only the new food. Monitor your dog's progress, and hopefully you'll see the beneficial effects of this weight-loss food.

Once the dog is on his new diet, under no circumstances should you give him other foods. This type of food is relatively high in indigestible fiber, which adds bulk to the food and makes your dog feel less hungry. Your dog's fecal output will increase as well.

Caution

Do not assume that because your dog is putting on weight it is because you have been overfeeding him and not giving him enough exercise. Your dog could have the condition known as hypothyroidism (see pages 130–31), which affects the thyroid gland. In older dogs, always arrange a veterinary checkup before starting a weight-loss program.

Home-Produced Food

If you are feeding your dog home-produced foods, it is often recommended to increase the vegetable content of the diet. Before making changes to your dog's diet, consult your veterinarian. Some vegetables, such as potatoes and sweet potatoes, are good sources of carbohydrate, which can add to the energy level of the diet. However, it is also common for flatulence to become a significant problem in dogs fed this type of diet. You can address this problem by giving your dog garlic pills or capsules, which may be disguised in the food (see pages 26–27). These are available in herbal veterinary products. Do not use fresh garlic, which can be toxic.

Breaking the Begging Habit

Instead of feeding your dog once or twice a day, try feeding him three or four smaller meals. To decrease the amount of begging at the dinner table, feed your dog before you feed your family. If there are other pets in the household, make sure you feed your overweight dog in a separate area—and be careful he doesn't try to eat the food put out for your other pets.

If your dog has been accustomed to regularly receiving treats as a reward for good behavior, he will continue to expect them. Instead of offering food, make a fuss over your pet when he behaves as required. If you must give your dog treats, make sure you cut out the calorie-laden ones and replace them with healthy options, such as a piece of carrot or apple, which are just as delicious.

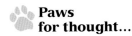

Paws for thought...

If an older dog is overweight or has arthritis, he may struggle—and may even find it painful—to bend down to reach his food and water. You can invest in a special eating table for dogs, which has holes in it for the dog's bowls.

Eating tables are available at various heights to suit dogs of different sizes.

Allergies and
Enzymes

Food allergies and intolerances can frequently emerge in dogs under two years old, but they may also arise unexpectedly in an older dog. The production of enzymes may also decrease in an older dog. Fortunately, these conditions can be easily addressed.

Although food allergies in dogs have attracted growing attention over recent years, it is not an easy area to investigate, and it is hard to reach conclusive answers. The main symptom of a food allergy is typically an irritation of the skin, which causes the dog to scratch repeatedly at its body, possibly injuring himself.

Susceptible Breeds

Any dog can be affected by a food allergy, but the problem often appears to be more closely associated with certain breeds than others. These include:

• West Highland white terriers (below)

• Dobermans

• Labrador retrievers

Finding an Allergy-Free Diet

If your dog experiences this allergic reaction, you'll need to change his diet. The reaction is probably linked to protein. Replace the protein ingredient of the diet—for example, beef—with an alternative, such as chicken, and see if the condition improves. It can take a month or longer to establish a concrete result.

Making such a dietary change usually means feeding your dog fresh food, which you should do under the supervision of your veterinarian. If you don't want to make fresh food for your dog, there are special commercially prepared diets available, which you can obtain from your veterinarian. However, it is often better to perform this trial with unprocessed foods in case there is another constituent in the diet that is the source of the problem.

Assuming that this switch in diet improves your dog's condition, you will need to avoid giving him that particular source of protein in the future. Once you've isolated the source of the allergen, you can obtain special hypoallergenic diets from some pet food manufacturers. These are based on protein sources, such as duck, which your dog is unlikely to have eaten regularly in the past, and will hopefully avoid any future flare-ups.

Gluten-Free Diets

It is not just animal protein that may have adverse effects on dogs. Although less common, there is evidence that dogs can develop gluten intolerance. Gluten is a protein present in various cereals—most notably wheat, rye, and barley—but not in rice or corn. Gluten intolerance often causes digestive disturbances, such as diarrhea and flatulence, which are similar to the symptoms of celiac disease in humans; however, skin problems can occur, too. To determine if these cereals are creating a problem, perform a similar test to the one recommended for animal protein allergies, but exclude grains instead of meat.

Repeated scratching is a possible sign that your dog may have developed an allergy to a component of his diet.

Gluten-free dog foods are now available. If you are preparing fresh food for your dog at home, choose a source of carbohydrate, such as rice or corn, that is not associated with gluten intolerance.

Enzymes and Bromelain

As a dog grows older, his ability to digest food can be reduced as a result of a drop in its enzymatic output. Enzymes are produced in the digestive system to help digest food. If there is a drop in enzyme production in your dog, a special enzyme supplement can be helpful. It helps to improve a dog's ability to break down food, as well as to ensure that key nutrients, such as zinc, are not lost from the body.

A natural substance known as bromelain, which is derived from pineapple, is especially recommended for older dogs. It contains proteases, which can assist in the breakdown of dietary proteins, and has other constituents that have anti-inflammatory effects. It may be helpful in countering arthritis as well as allergies. There are now specially formulated enzymatic supplements containing bromelain on the market for dogs. However, bromelain needs to be used in moderation because it has other effects that can be harmful, such as thinning of the blood.

Natural Remedies

Some enzymatic components, including lipases (a component from the plant *Aspergillus oryzae*), improve the digestion of fats. These are available from health food stores, but seek veterinary advice before giving them to your dog.

CHAPTER 4 Playful
as a Pup

Your dog will exercise less as he grows older, but this doesn't mean that you should stop taking him out for a walk once or twice every day. Exercising your dog outside his home surroundings will aid his mental alertness as well as his fitness. Even an elderly dog enjoys playing—chasing after a ball, perhaps— although not with the same vigor as when he was younger. Your observations will be important in assessing what exercise your older dog can manage. Be prepared to adjust your dog's routine to make it more suitable for your pet.

Getting Enough
Exercise

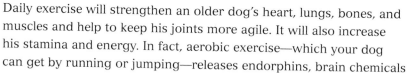

Ensuring that your dog has plenty of exercise will help your pet stay healthy for as long as possible, keep his weight under control to avoid obesity, and stimulate his mental alertness—overall, making him a more content, happy dog. However, too much exercise can have undesirable effects, so make sure you don't push your dog too much.

A daily outing in the park provides Millie, an aging golden retriever, plenty of exercise.

Daily exercise will strengthen an older dog's heart, lungs, bones, and muscles and help to keep his joints more agile. It will also increase his stamina and energy. In fact, aerobic exercise—which your dog can get by running or jumping—releases endorphins, brain chemicals that will cause your dog to feel happy. An exercised dog will be less bored, too, so he will be less likely to chew your sneakers and bark.

Exercise will help to ensure that your dog does not start to become overweight. It can also play a role in preventing certain diseases, such as arthritis, heart disease, respiratory problems, and gastrointestinal diseases. Even if your dog has a health problem, such as a heart ailment, regular exercise will help to improve his cardiac function—but in such a case, always follow the advice of your veterinarian.

How Much is Enough?

Different breeds of dog will vary in their exercise requirements. Those that have been bred for working purposes before becoming popular as pets, such as Labrador retrievers, have considerably more stamina than lapdogs, such as the Pekingese, which were originally bred as companions. However, size alone is not a true reflection of the amount of exercise that a breed will require. Some small dogs, such as terriers, have a working ancestry, and this is reflected in their active natures—terriers often display considerable stamina for their size. Conversely, not all large dogs will need long walks. For example, greyhounds generally prefer running for a relatively short period of time.

Preparing for the Outdoors

Just as people should warm up before exercising and cool down afterward, dogs should, too. You should bend and stretch your dog's limbs for a few minutes before exercising and start at a slow pace. When you're nearing the end of the exercise period, encourage your dog to slow down again. You can finish off with a massage (see pages 66–67).

The best time to take your dog out for exercise depends on the weather. In hot weather take your dog out in the early morning and late afternoon when the weather is normally cooler to protect him from the risk of heatstroke (see page 33). If the sun is strong, there is also a risk that a dog can suffer from sunburn (see page 18). In cold or wet weather it is advisable to exercise an older dog in a coat (see pages 32–33).

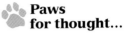

Paws for thought...

If your dog seems tired or starts to have difficulty covering the normal distance of a walk, it's usually simply a matter of cutting back on the length of the walk. Nevertheless, a veterinary checkup is also a wise precaution— just in case a specific medical condition is responsible for this change in behavior.

Case History

A New Life for Monty

Monty, an overweight bulldog, was taken by his owner to an animal shelter because he was being destructive and kept stealing food. Fortunately, he was given a new home. To help Monty become fit, his new owners placed him on a strict diet and gradually increased his level of exercise. This regime has had another benefit: Monty has stopped being destructive. Because Monty is taken out regularly for a walk, he is no longer left at home all day on his own, being bored—in the past, this boredom had led him to search for something to amuse himself, such as chewing a slipper. The exercise is also helping Monty to sleep better.

Going for a
Healthy Walk

 **Paws
for thought...**

It is better to walk
a small dog using a
harness instead of a
collar. It helps to ease
the pressure on the
neck by dispersing it
over the shoulders and
lessens the likelihood
of disk problems (see
pages 118–19).

**Walking is an ideal form of exercise for most dogs. The
amount of walking suitable for your dog—whether trotting
alongside you at a leisurely pace or running at bursts of
speed—will depend on his breed. Walking should be an
enjoyable experience for both you and your dog.**

When you take your dog for a walk, he will probably exercise
naturally within his own safety limits. In general, especially for an
elderly dog, it is best to provide two short walks every day instead
of a single, longer outing. This will reduce the risk of overtiring your
pet. Veterinarians usually recommend about 15 to 20 minutes for each
walk. You should avoid long walks, which may aggravate underlying
joint ailments and risks straining muscles, too.

Taking Your Dog to the Park

Most dogs love going to the park because to them it's an exciting
place full of stimuli. Although it may seem repetitive to you to walk
in the same park every day, there are often new dogs for your dog
to meet, as well as dogs that your pet will recognize from previous
encounters. There will also be new scents for a dog to investigate.

Remember that not all dogs in a park are friendly or well-controlled.
An older dog is usually more vulnerable to being attacked by an

A portable drinking aid,
available from pet centers,
is ideal for making sure
your dog has plenty of
water at all times.

aggressive dog, because an older dog is less agile, so
he will not be as quick at avoiding an assault as in the
past. When other dogs are around, try keeping your
dog close to you so that you can intervene immediately
if an aggressive encounter appears imminent.

Taking your dog regularly to a park where other dogs
congregate will introduce the risk of his picking up
an infection. This is particularly true for an older dog
because his immune system will be impaired by age
and won't be able to provide the same protection as
when he was younger. Therefore, it is important to

ensure that your pet's vaccinations are up to date to protect him from serious diseases (see pages 16–17).

Venturing Farther Away

You can take your dog into the countryside for a walk, but remember that an older dog may tire more easily in these surroundings, especially if the ground is steep or uneven. If you are planning to be out for any length of time, do not forget to take some water for your pet to drink. This is particularly important for an older dog—he is at greater risk of dehydration because his kidneys cannot concentrate urine to the same extent as when he was younger. You can purchase a specially designed, portable drinking container that converts into a bowl for your dog. These can be hung from your belt or have a strap to carry them across your shoulders.

In unfamiliar surroundings, you should keep a close watch on your dog, particularly if he likes to wander away. Along with its other senses, a dog's hearing declines with age, so your dog may have greater difficulty finding his way back to you if you are separated, especially when twilight approaches. It is a good idea to keep your dog on a leash after dark if he has a tendency to stray off.

Two's Company

As a dog becomes older, some owners acquire a young puppy to keep the older dog company and to encourage him to stay active. However, while puppies need only restricted exercise, like older dogs, this stage will pass within a year or so. The younger dog will need much more exercise than his aging companion, which can make it difficult to arrange their exercising routines. To avoid this problem, choose a new dog whose exercise requirements are naturally more limited. For example, a greyhound can be an ideal match for an older Labrador retriever.

!

Caution

Avoid allowing a zealous dog, such as a terrier, to overdo things. Watch out for signs that signal it's time to stop—when your dog seems tired or is breathing hard, with his sides heaving.

When out for a walk, the younger dog chases a ball for exercise while the older companion strolls along.

Exercise and
Swimming

One great form of exercise for dogs is swimming. Most dogs can swim well by using their legs to paddle and their tail to steer through the water. Hydrotherapy, where exercise takes place in water, is also beneficial for dogs.

Some dogs are more suited for the water than others. Newfoundlands and Labrador retrievers are naturally drawn to water because they were bred to work in and around it. They will plunge into ponds and other stretches of water if the opportunity arises. However, other dogs, such as basset hounds, are more reluctant to take the plunge.

Swimmers vs. Landlubbers

Great Swimmers

- Curly-coated retriever
- Irish water spaniel
- Labrador retriever
- Newfoundland
- Standard poodle

Reluctant Swimmers

- Dachshund
- Basset hound
- Mexican hairless
- Pekingese
- Whippet

Splashing in the water is a favorite activity for many dogs—including Madison, a retriever that enjoys fetching playthings from the water.

Swimming is an effective way of improving a dog's muscle tone. The basic movement of swimming is similar to walking and utilizes the same muscles. However, the water supports the dog's weight, so unlike with walking, there is nothing that will foster joint pain. In addition, the muscles do more work to counter the weight of the water. The pressure of water on the chest also makes the muscles used for breathing work harder, especially on inspiration, while the heart gets a workout by pumping more blood around the body.

Inland Dangers

A calm pond or small lake is normally a safe place for most dogs to swim, but make sure there is a suitable area for your dog to climb out of the water. An older, less agile dog encounters greater difficulties in leaving the water than a younger dog and can drown.

Avoid taking your dog near a fast-flowing river, or even a canal, in case he plunges into the water. He may have difficulties in leaving the water, and an older dog will tire more easily, especially if there are strong currents. If your route takes you past potentially dangerous stretches of water, place your dog on his leash beforehand.

At the Beach

Dogs often splash around in the surf at a beach instead of swimming. This can be good exercise, but if the weather is cool, take a towel with you so that you can rub down your dog afterward to prevent him from becoming chilled. It is also important to take a supply of fresh drinking water—and make sure your dog does not drink salt water. This can lead to vomiting, and its high sodium content will worsen an underlying kidney condition or high blood pressure.

Canine Hydrotherapy

Hydrotherapy provides the same benefits of swimming, and for an older dog with a joint ailment, it can help to maintain and improve the dog's fitness and mobility and provide pain relief. Hydrotherapy takes place in heated pools with a water temperature of 75–86°F (24–30°C). This encourages blood flow to the skin, so the muscles can work more efficiently. A weekly session is usually recommended for a dog with arthritis and entails a five-minute swim in the beginning.

Choosing a Hydrotherapy Center

When deciding on a hydrotherapy center for your dog, consider the following:

- Get a recommendation from your veterinarian for a treatment pool in your area; he should help to coordinate your pet's treatment.

- Look for a pool with high standards of hygiene. The water quality should be monitored throughout the day to minimize the risk of infection.

- Make sure the pool has a safety certification and is insured.

- Ensure the operator keeps detailed records of your dog's treatment.

Tools for
Playtime

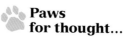 **Paws
for thought…**

Instead of bringing a toy
with you when you take
your dog for a walk, you
can encourage him to
use his senses with a
variation on hide-and-
seek. First disappear
behind a tree, then call
your dog to you.

**An important part of keeping your dog motivated is to add
some variety to his exercise routine by including toys and
games. Some of these are ideal for taking with you when
visiting a park; others are suitable for playing with in the
home. All will contribute to your dog's mental alertness.**

Old dogs retain their playful instincts from puppyhood, so try taking
a toy with you when you go walking. It will encourage your dog to
run more, and he will cover more ground as he runs ahead to collect
the toy and bring it back to you. Playing games with your dog will
also help to maintain his coordination and mental alertness.

You should bear in mind your dog's general state of health when
choosing toys for him. If your dog has painful joints, for example, a
flying disk—which will encourage your dog to jump up to catch it in
the air—will be less suitable. In such a case, it is better
to roll a ball along the ground toward your dog
so he can pick up the ball and bring it back to
you. Avoid throwing a ball into the distance
for your dog to chase as he did when he
was younger—you don't want him to
overstretch himself. Try to throw your
dog's toy in an area where there will
be no risk of it being taken by another
dog, which can lead to conflict. Also
remember that it is never a good idea
to throw a stick for your dog. It can cause
injury if the dog misjudges his leap and is
hit in the mouth or face.

Toys and Games at Home
Be prepared to invest in several toys
because dogs differ in their preferences.
Fabric toys are ideal for indoor play, where

A "bone" made with
two tennis balls is
great for retrieving.

they will stay relatively clean. Plastic toys can be played with inside or outdoors—and it is easy to wash the mud off them.

An older dog can benefit from toys that he can chew long after he has finished teething. They can help to clean his teeth (see pages 28–31), although they are not a substitute for regular brushing. They will also help to keep an older dog occupied. Try hiding your dog's favorite toy so he can have the thrill of hunting for it. Alternatively, if you are feeding your dog dry food, try hiding the food for your dog to find—you can leave a trail of food to the bowl if your dog's senses of smell and vision are declining.

If you have a dog with wide jaws, such as a bull terrier, who prefers tug-of-war, make sure to play gently. An older dog has delicate jaws and teeth, and the tugging action can cause injury.

Stay Away from My Toys

If you have a female dog that has not been spayed, she may act strange and display an attachment to her toys about eight weeks after her last season has finished. She may growl and lunge aggressively at you if you try to take them away. This is a common manifestation of a false, or pseudo-, pregnancy. The dog's mammary glands may be swollen and leak milk. These symptoms are caused by hormonal changes within the body, suggesting that the dog was pregnant—however, in reality, this was not the case. The dog will view her toys as her puppies, which is why she is protective toward them.

This phase will pass in a few weeks, but she will probably suffer from further false pregnancies and the symptoms may become progressively worse. The best solution—assuming that the dog is otherwise in good health—will be to have her spayed. This prevents any further seasons, thus eliminating the problem.

Teeth-friendly retrieving toy

Knotted rope for playing fetch or tug-of-war

Rubber toy in which you can hide treats

Rubber ball with handle for throwing

The Benefits of
Massage

The benefits of exercise should not stop when you arrive home. Exercise improves the circulation, and by following it with a massage, you can loosen the muscle fibers that may have become taut and enhance the feeling of well-being that comes with exercise.

5 Steps to a Massage

For the best results, follow these steps when giving your dog a massage:

1. Place your dog so he is at a height that is comfortable for you, without excessive stooping. You may need to place him on a table covered with a cloth or blanket. You can massage a smaller dog on your lap.

2. Choose a quiet environment where there are no distractions, such as another dog in the room. Speak softly and reassuringly to help your dog overcome any anxieties.

3. Do not be surprised if, at first, your dog wriggles about and wants to get down onto the floor. Persevere gently, stroking your dog to help him relax. Before long, your pet should settle down, particularly if he has just been exercising and is tired.

4. Begin the massage. Concentrate on what your fingers are telling you. You may notice areas of the body that are warm or slightly swollen, which may indicate inflammation.

5. Be careful about how much pressure you apply, and take particular care if your dog has painful joints; otherwise, you may hurt him. Be alert to any signs of pain, such as a sudden movement from your dog.

As long as your dog doesn't have a broken bone or other painful injury, it is easy to give him a massage. You will need only five minutes, so it is not a time-consuming routine—but you can massage your dog for longer if you like. Stroking your dog and massaging him will reinforce the bond between you and your pet; however, massage entails more clearly defined movements on your part and normally involves applying more pressure to the body. It demands greater sensitivity, too.

Starting the Massage

Develop a routine that suits both you and your dog, following the points in 5 Steps to a Massage (left). Keep the sessions short at first, about five minutes. Depending on your dog's temperament, you can extend them for up to 30 minutes.

Start with gentle movements and increase pressure gradually, using a regular rhythmic flow. Observe how your dog is reacting. Constant hand contact is important to help your dog relax. Develop a contact frequency of about once a second. Do not apply only your fingertips. Although they are the most sensitive part of the hand for you to feel feedback, because they are packed with nerve endings, to give an effective massage you need to use the entire hand, including the palms.

Types of Massage Movements

Effleurage is probably the most important massage stroke, especially in old dogs, because it aids the circulation of both blood and lymph. (For this same reason, massage may not be recommended for a dog with cancer—blood can help a tumor to grow.) It can be useful for dogs with congestive heart failure. Effleurage entails using the hands to glide over the dog's body in the direction of the heart. Use your whole hand on the dog's body; however, concentrate on using the palm of the hand on the dog's legs, working up and never down each limb. The rate of the massage will influence its impact. Strokes every three seconds are soothing, as well as beneficial within the body.

Petrissage comprises different basic massage techniques, which collectively are valuable in treating muscle tension. This is often linked with conditions associated with old age, such as arthritis, where the pain from the joint causes the nearby muscles to become stiff and painful, thereby worsening the handicap. Some petrissage movements include kneading and squeezing the muscle mass by applying pressure and then relaxing. You can also lift and gently roll the dog's skin to help tone the skin and the layers beneath.

When massaging, make sure your dog is comfortable, perhaps providing a towel.

Weighing In

Before you massage your dog, test how powerful your hands are by pressing them on a bathroom scale. This will help you gauge the amount of pressure to apply to your dog. In most cases you should only use pressure equivalent to ½–20 pounds (0.23–9.1kg). If you exceed this figure, you may cause bruising to your dog.

Helping Your Dog
Avoid Injury

Caution

If you try to lift your dog and he growls, this is a serious warning. He may be in pain and may bite you. Try to adjust your hold to find a more comfortable position when lifting your dog, or depending on the situation, you may have to use a muzzle.

A child's gate prevents Milo, a Jack Russell terrier with short legs, from climbing stairs.

Your dog may not be as active as he used to be, but he is still at risk of injuring himself, especially if he becomes overexcited. Your dog may not realize that he cannot do everything that he used to do as a puppy—it's up to you to ensure that he stays safe.

One of the most common ways for an older dog to injure himself is by jumping, and you'll need to remember this both in the home and when outdoors. It doesn't matter if the distance of the jump is great or small—it is the impact of landing, or an awkward landing, that will cause the damage. This is why rolling a ball on a ground is better for an older dog than throwing it up into the air, which encourages him to jump up. For the same reason, it is best to avoid throwing a flying disk for your dog to catch in the air.

Jumping up, such as over a fence or other obstacle, is often worse than jumping down, because the dog may fail to appreciate the decline in his athletic ability and will not be able to jump high enough to clear the hurdle. If your dog then collides with a hard surface, he may scrape his legs or fall awkwardly, which will put stress on the joints and the ligaments supporting them.

Indoor Hurdles

Unfortunately, it will be more difficult to prevent your dog from jumping up onto your furniture, especially if he is used to sleeping on a favorite chair or couch. Be prepared to lift your dog more frequently as necessary. Bear in mind that a dog that has not been used to being handled in this way may at first resent it. This applies particularly if your dog has any type of joint pain affecting his hips, because you will need to lift the dog around his hindquarters to support his weight (see *3 Steps to Lifting Your Dog Safely,* right).

Avoiding Stairs

It is important to dissuade any dog that has had a prolapsed disk (see pages 118–19), or that belongs in a high-risk category, such as breeds with short legs—particularly dachshunds—from attempting to climb up stairs. Although a prolapsed disk can strike at any stage in life, the prognosis is particularly poor in an older dog. Repeated occurrences of this condition are common in breeds prone to the problem, and climbing stairs is a typical way for a prolapsed disk to occur. To protect your dog, you can invest in a child's gate, which is normally used to deter toddlers from venturing up or down stairs.

Getting Your Dog into a Vehicle

Even if your dog has always cleared the tailgate easily when he was younger, now that he is older do not encourage him to jump up into the back of a vehicle. Instead, you may be able to lift your dog up to place him inside. However, this can be difficult with a large, heavy dog—and you may want to avoid having your clothes covered in mud and hair, too. Many vehicle manufacturers are aware of this problem, and you might be able to obtain a special ramp, which will allow your dog to walk up from the ground into the back of a vehicle.

To lift a larger dog, such as Sally, make sure you bend and lift from your knees, not your back, to avoid injurying yourself.

Ramp Use

Initially, your dog may think the ramp is a great opportunity for playing a game; conversely, he may be nervous about going up the ramp. However, you should soon be able to persuade your dog to enter the vehicle using a ramp without difficulty. To prevent your dog from jumping off, lead him up the ramp while keeping the leash relatively tight, with the dog near you. Remain alert and be ready to use your spare hand to give support if the dog seems to want to stray off the ramp. If your pet has taken part in agility competitions

3 Steps to Lifting Your Dog Safely

Follow these steps to lift your dog with the least amount of discomfort:

1. Bend down from your knees to a comfortable height, and place your left arm around the front of your dog's body.

2. Then place your other arm around your dog's hindquarters.

3. Gently lift up your dog, allowing the weight of his body to rest on your arms. Don't let your dog hang down—this will not only be uncomfortable, it can also injure your dog.

For a heavy dog, such as Buster, the best way to get him in and out of a car is to let him use a ramp.

Caution

If placing your dog in a crate, take his leash off to prevent it from becoming tangled while traveling, and ensure the door is properly closed to prevent any accidents on the journey.

when he was younger, he should be able to adapt to using a ramp without any difficulty because of his past training.

A Small-Scale Solution

Ramps are useful for large dogs, but for small dogs it will be more convenient and easier to use a carrying crate, in which your dog can travel. You can simply lift the crate in and out of the vehicle.

Securely position the crate in the vehicle so that it cannot be thrown about if you apply the brakes suddenly. Commercially available crates are made in various sizes. You should ensure that a crate not only accommodates your dog but also fits easily into your vehicle. Crates are ideal for using in hatchbacks or sport-utility vehicles because they can often be fitted in place behind the back seat instead of on the seat. When not in use, these crates should collapse easily for storage in the vehicle.

Special Precautions When Out and About

When taking your dog out for exercise, whether young or old, there is always a risk of injury or an accident. However, because an older dog is less agile and may be losing his sight and hearing, there are certain situations in which you need to be particularly cautious.

Take care when walking your dog near traffic, especially once he is elderly. The risk period is not necessarily when your dog is off the leash—you should choose an area away from danger before removing it. Walking down the road with your pet, especially if the sidewalk is narrow, can be dangerous if your dog strays slightly on the leash and steps out into the path of a vehicle. Make sure you always remain alert to this possibility. If your dog is becoming deaf or if his vision is becoming impaired, he may not hear or see an approaching car. For the same reasons, also take care when walking down a rural road.

Countryside Danger

When taking your dog for a country outing, be more cautious of the surroundings (see page 61)—and other animals, such as snakes, skunks, porcupines, and badgers, depending on where you live. An older dog's senses are diminished and his reflexes are slower. For example, an older dog is more likely to be bitten by a venomous snake than a younger dog, either because he fails to see the reptile or because he can't jump away quickly enough to avoid the snake.

The risk period is greatest early in the morning, particularly in spring in temperate areas, where snakes are emerging from hibernation. The air temperature makes the snakes more sluggish during this period, so instead of slithering away undetected, the snake is more tempted to lunge at the dog. You may not notice right away what has happened, but your dog will have almost immediate difficulty walking. On close inspection, you may see two puncture marks from the snake's fangs.

3 Steps to Take for a Snake Bite

If a snake bites your dog, he will need veterinary help quickly. Follow the points below—they will give you the greatest chance of saving your dog's life:

1. If you can, identify the snake or note its markings—but only do so without putting yourself in danger.

2. Carry your dog to your vehicle. Try to keep him as quiet as possible to help avoid spreading the snake's venom.

3. If available, use a phone to call your veterinary practice to alert it about the emergency before you arrive.

Note: Applying a tourniquet is controversial because if applied incorrectly the leg can become gangrenous and need amputating.

For late outings, invest in a glow-in-the-dark collar so that you and others can see your dog.

Improving
Mobility

Canine physiotherapy is becoming increasingly important in helping a dog with a physical injury or condition, such as osteoarthritis, joint and ligament injuries, hip and elbow dysplasia, and back pain. Whether a short-term or lifelong problem, it can help a dog to retain his maximum mobility and improve his quality of life, even if he is elderly.

There are a variety of techniques and aids used in this type of treatment, depending on the problem. These include hydrotherapy (see pages 62–63) and massage (see pages 66–67) and techniques to mobilize the soft tissues and joints, as well as specific exercises.

Getting Around on Wheels

Even dogs that have severe hind-limb paralysis can be encouraged to get exercise. Special carts equipped with wheels, which support a dog's hind legs as he pulls it along, are available. Although the hindquarters will not be exercised, other muscles, including those in the dog's front limbs, will be. It is remarkable how quickly a dog can adapt to this new form of locomotion. Obviously, you should try to exercise your dog on relatively level ground.

A cart and harness allows partly paralyzed Ralphie to enjoy short walks with his owner.

Ultrasound, neuromuscular stimulators, and pulsed magnetic field therapy are procedures that may also be used. Specially trained physiotherapists work alongside veterinarians to ensure a coordinated treatment plan, which may involve only one form of treatment or a combination. The goal will be to reduce pain and improve mobility.

Physiotherapy for the Injured

If physiotherapy is given because of an injury or surgery, the treatment will help your dog return to pre-injury strength and mobility, as well as prevent a reoccurrence of the injury. One common technique is so-called "bicycling," performed with the dog lying on his back. This procedure allows the dog's limbs to be manipulated to resemble the way in which they operate when he is moving freely on his own. It is a useful way to maintain muscle tone, especially after surgery. The prevention of muscle wasting, or "atrophy," is important because it will ensure that the dog starts walking again with less difficulty after a minimum period of incapacity.

A special harness enables Jackson, who has a hip problem, to climb up steps.

Physiotherapy for Paralyzed Dogs

If the dog is paralyzed, physiotherapy techniques play an important role in helping to maintain the dog's muscle tone. These include the so-called "towel-walking" technique, where the dog is placed in a sling, which supports the majority of his weight while his feet are in contact with the ground. The resistance that passes up through the toes has a direct impact on the dog's muscles, helping to keep them relatively strong. This is in spite of the fact that the dog may not be able to use his muscles to walk, because they are not receiving nerve impulses from the spinal cord.

In a case where a dog's back legs are permanently paralyzed, towel walking can be used in conjunction with fitting a cart to the dog's hindquarters, which provides the dog with some mobility (see *Getting Around on Wheels,* left).

Amputation

Giant breeds, such as Irish wolfhounds, are vulnerable to bone tumors in later life, which may require the amputation of an affected leg. However, most dogs are adaptable, and the effects of this disability are minimal.

Exercise plays an important role in aiding recovery and helping to increase the muscle mass in the opposite limb. If your dog has a leg amputated, allow an initial period of adjustment. Avoid places where you may meet a lot of other dogs until your pet has adapted to getting about on three legs.

CHAPTER

5 Teaching an Old Dog New Tricks

As a dog grows older, his pattern of behavior alters due to the physical changes caused by aging. The changes are gradual, however, so you may not notice them initially. But by the time he is elderly, your dog's mental faculties may be noticeably weaker.

In the past, there was little that could be done to improve the condition of an elderly dog with age-related mental deterioration. However, there are drugs available now that can help in many cases, and at a relatively modest cost. Even so, it is not just simply a matter of reaching for a container of pills; you can play an important part in keeping your pet mentally alert by providing him with an occasional new toy or changing where you walk. These are both excellent ways to keep your dog stimulated.

A Dog's Changing
Personality

As a dog ages he will become less agile and develop medical problems, and his senses will begin to fail, too. These emotional and physical changes can change a dog's personality. Some become more mellow, others nervous or grumpy.

Like people, a dog's personality can change as he becomes older. Although some dogs will remain boisterous and show signs of the energy they had as puppies, other dogs become more peaceful and docile. As a dog matures, he may become more settled with his position in his "human pack" and will no longer need to prove his rank. Conversely, a dog with a nervous disposition, perhaps scared of thunderstorms, may become even more nervous as he ages.

The Demanding Dog

Some dogs become more demanding of their owner's time. They need more reassurance and may become dependent and fussy. They may even become anxious, clinging to you and following you around the house. If this is the case with your dog, you probably don't spend enough time with him or provide him with enough attention and physical contact. Depending on your relationship with your dog, this additional need for social contact can be seen as a plus or a minus. If you provide more social contact, your dog will become more confident and less anxious. However, be careful not to respond to his demands for attention—he needs to know that you are still the boss.

The Grumpy Dog

Many dogs become more docile with age, but some dogs become grumpy and prefer much less interaction with people. If not left alone, they can even become aggressive, perhaps growling or snapping at their owners. If your dog is grumpy and aggressive simply because he prefers to be

A nervous dog, such as 9-year-old Muffin, will enjoy the physical contact provided by her owner.

Plenty of attention has made Molly, an 8-year-old golden retriever, a more confident dog, although she still needs to look to her owner for reassurance.

alone, allow him all the time for himself that he needs—but it is important to be sure that he has no associated health problems.

A dog that becomes irritable, stubborn, or aggressive might be experiencing a medical condition that is making him uncomfortable. If you notice such a change in your dog's behavior, bring him to the veterinarian for a checkup (see pages 16–17). It can be difficult to determine the precise cause of a behavioral problem in an older dog, simply because there can be a number of different illnesses involved, as well as an age-related loss of mental acuity.

It might be obvious that aging joints will make it more difficult for your dog to go on long walks (see pages 60–61). However, not all dog owners recognize that these painful joints can also take a toll on a dog's behavior in the home. He may be reluctant to climb up stairs or jump up onto a chair. He may also decline from letting young children give him hugs—even if he once had a docile nature. Let your dog's reactions guide you in how you handle him. You may need to carry him up the stairs (see pages 68–69) or provide a more comfortable sleeping arrangement (see page 19).

The Defensive Dog

As a dog ages, he usually becomes less territorial—but in some cases a dog will become more territorial and defensive. Just as an older person may lose his temper more quickly, an older dog that normally has a defensive nature may bark or display other signs of defending more quickly. His territory—your home—becomes more important, and strangers become more of a threat. This behavior may start to decline as the dog's hearing fails; visitors at the front door will not be noticed because he can no longer hear footsteps approaching the door or a ringing doorbell.

Scatter a few dog beds around the house if your dog prefers to nap with you nearby.

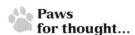

Paws for thought…

A male dog that was once difficult to keep away from females is often less troublesome when older. This is due to a drop in testosterone levels. He also won't be agile enough to scale fences in pursuit of the object of his amorous attentions—and his back legs may not be strong enough to support his weight during mating.

No matter the reason for your dog's grumpiness, avoid situations that can cause him to act aggressively. For example, if you have friends over for dinner or you plan to have babies and toddlers in the house, keep your dog in a room out of bounds to your visitors. The older dog tends to be less adaptable to changes in his environment, too. If you make any changes to your home or its surroundings, this may lead to behavioral difficulties in your dog.

New Sleeping Patterns

Just as an older person experiences a change in sleeping pattern—usually sleeping in short spells and less often—an older dog will have a change in sleeping pattern, too. The older dog usually sleeps more often throughout the day, and this need for more sleep increases with each year. However, if your dog develops a clinging nature toward you, he might only become relaxed enough to sleep when you are seated, when he knows you'll be in one place for some time. Even if he is desperate for a nap, he may not take one unless you're next to him. If your dog develops this habit, provide him with several beds throughout the house. Once he does fall asleep, you can tiptoe away quietly. If you need to leave your dog alone, you can leave some old shirts with your scent on them in the beds to provide reassurance.

Not Responding to Your Whistles?

Just as a person's senses may become less acute with age, the same is true for a dog. You'll most likely to notice this when whistling for your dog. If he is not as responsive as he used to be, don't think your dog is becoming stubborn—he may not be able to hear as well, especially because whistles have a high frequency. Although dogs can hear sounds that are inaudible to our ears, this ability declines with age. Try calling your dog back to you instead of using a whistle; he will be more likely to respond. Hand signals may also help.

Failing Eyes

You might start hearing noises in the night if your dog starts to have difficulty finding his way around after dark. It is not unusual for a dog's eyes to turn cloudy with age, thus weakening his ability to see.

In certain cases, this can be a symptom of a specific genetic disease known as progressive retinal atrophy (PRA; see pages 124–25). Your dog may be able to find his way around in familiar surroundings because he can remember the layout of your home. However, if you alter the position of the furniture in a room, your dog might bump into it, causing you to think that he has suddenly become clumsy. If your dog does seem to be clumsy all of a sudden, you should bring him to a veterinarian to determine the cause of the problem.

Changes in your dog's hearing and vision can cause your dog to become more aggressive. If he cannot hear or see what is approaching him, he may become more fearful because he has no warning. In these circumstances, you'll need to make sure you approach your dog so that he's not frightened.

Your Response

An owner's reaction can also have an impact on a dog's behavior. For example, an elderly dog that has kidney failure may start to urinate around the home. If he is repeatedly scolded or even chastised by his owner, he may display signs of a nervous disorder, such as starting to regularly bite at his skin. Conversely, allowing an undesirable habit to develop in an older dog unchecked can create difficulties, too.

It is important to take a fair and consistent view of your dog's behavior. Seek advice from your veterinarian, who may refer your dog to a behaviorist to remedy anything that is a cause for concern before it develops into a troublesome habit.

Using hand signals is a good way to communicate with your dog if he has hearing problems.

Dealing with
Poor Behavior

As your dog enters old age, you may become aware of an apparent breakdown in his training. Although this can be distressing at times, try not to get upset with your dog if he fails to respond or apparently misbehaves.

Relentless barking while a dog's owner is not at home can be a sign of separation anxiety.

If there is a change in your dog's behavior, it could be an indication of an underlying medical problem, such as canine cognitive dysfunction (CCD; see pages 122–23) or another condition, or it could be the result of an emotional change.

Separation Anxiety

Some dogs develop a phobia about being left alone in the home for any period of time. You may not be aware of this problem until a neighbor mentions your dog has been barking or howling while you're away, unless your pet becomes destructive around the home, too. In some cases a dog may run around the house and try to escape by digging frantically at a door, injuring his paws and mouth during the process. This behavior stems back to the pack instincts that developed from the dog's ancestor, the wolf. A domestic dog sees itself as part of a family group. If he worries that he has lost contact with his family and feels isolated, he barks or howls to call them.

Barking can develop into a noisy habit and may lead to complaints from neighbors. To avoid this problem, try varying the length of time in which you are away from home, making some absences short, others longer. When you need to go out for longer, always try to exercise your dog first so that he will want to sleep while you are away. Change your routine before you leave home. If you normally put on your coat and then pick up your keys, pick up the keys first. While you are away from home, leave some old, unwashed clothes with your scent on them in your dog's bed to provide reassurance, and try leaving the radio or television on. In the short term your veterinarian may prescribe an antianxiety medication to help your pet. This can be important if your dog is barking repeatedly over long periods.

Sleep-Related Disorders

If your dog does not sleep at night, try to reinforce his natural sleeping pattern by keeping him awake as much as possible during the day and taking him out for a walk just before turning in at night. This should bring his natural body clock back into relative harmony.

It is also important to avoid conditioning your pet into an attention-seeking mode, where he knows that he can attract your attention simply by barking at night. The longer it lasts, the harder it will be to overcome.

Disharmony

In a few cases, there may come a time when two dogs that have always lived together in harmony will begin to disagree. This often occurs among assertive dogs—including sled breeds, such as the husky—where a strong hierarchal dominance is present, and particularly when the dogs are both unneutered males. It reflects what happens in the wolf pack when an older dominant member of the group is challenged by a younger rival. Try to avoid potential flash points, such as mealtimes, by feeding the dogs separately, and concentrate on giving more attention to the older dog to help reinforce his dominance. In general, these disputes usually settle down without major conflict.

If you decide to introduce a young puppy to your home alongside an older dog that has already been established there, you should do so before the older dog loses his desire to play. Introductions should be relatively trouble-free—provided that you do not inadvertently undermine the position of your older dog. Make sure you give the older dog plenty of attention. And ensure the puppy has adequate exercise, too, so that it will not persist in wanting to play with its older companion.

The Anxious Dog

Sometimes a dog that was a little anxious as a puppy becomes more anxious as he ages. For example, a dog that might have been only slightly concerned about a noisy thunderstorm as a puppy may now hide, howl, or stay close to you—he might even panic, and tremble or run around the house. Bring your dog to the veterinarian to rule out any physical problems.

When the thunderstorm or other trigger approaches, try distracting your dog by playing a game or giving him a massage. Make sure you don't pamper your dog or try to calm him—this will only reward your dog for his behavior.

Paws for thought...

As a dog's hearing starts to decline, he will often start to bark because he is disoriented. It may help to play calming music at low volume to the dog—the background sound can help produce a soothing effect.

From Housebroken to
Accident-Prone

Provide plenty of water for older dogs—and ensure they have frequent trips outdoors to prevent an accident from occurring.

Caution
If your dog has an illness that predisposes him to drink more, and he is consequently producing more urine, the obvious solution may seem to be to reduce the amount of water you provide for him. However, you should never cut back on his water—this can have a catastrophic impact on his health.

The most alarming sign of aging is when a dog begins to have accidents around the house. In most cases, with appropriate care, problems with housebreaking can be resolved—at least in the short term.

An accident in the house may be because your dog has difficulty in getting outside, possibly because of a loss of mobility or pain. This explains why male dogs that used to cock their legs often start to do so less enthusiastically as they grow older, sometimes even preferring to squat like a female dog.

With a smaller dog, it may be possible to train him to use a litter tray, just like a cat. There are also special absorbent mats that can be used in the case of a larger dog. However, the best choice is to encourage your dog to go outside. Dogs are clean animals by nature, so if you place a dog that has previously been housebroken outside—even if you have to do so every hour or so—he should soon learn to respond and take advantage of the opportunity.

Cleanliness Counts
It is important to clean up thoroughly if your dog has soiled in the home. Otherwise, he will be drawn back to the same area again, setting up a cycle that will become progressively harder to break. Avoid using general household disinfectants that smell of ammonia to clean the area, because their smell will reinforce the appeal of the area. Instead, use a disinfectant specifically designed to clean pet accidents, which are sold in pet stores. There are also special de-scenting preparations available to remove any trace of the dog's odor from the area.

Diaper Control
If your dog is suffering from a loss of bladder tone and has become incontinent, you can try to make the situation more manageable by obtaining special gender-specific diapers for dogs from a pet store.

If they are not available in your area, you can purchase them over the Internet. You will need to care for your dog in the same way as a baby: Change the diaper frequently, and clean your dog's skin regularly using baby wipes.

Watch out for signs of any rash or other inflammation of the skin, which is usually the result of the acidic urine. In severe cases your veterinarian may recommend using an artificial barrier cream applied to vulnerable areas of the skin, where it dries. It guards against the impact of both urine and fecal material, thereby reducing the risk of infection. At night your dog can also sleep on a special absorbent pet bed, which will help to keep him dry.

The Underlying Problem

There are a number of causes for a relapse in housebreaking. Some of these conditions can be treated more easily than others. It is important to consult your veterinarian, who will be able to help unravel the cause and find a solution. In some cases, the problem may be due to a combination of factors. They include:

- A urinary infection (see page 91).
- Chronic kidney failure (see pages 94–97).
- Cushing's disease (see pages 131).
- Diabetes (see pages 134–37).
- Canine cognitive dysfunction (see pages 122–23).
- A lack of estrogen in older female dogs.
- Lack of mobility.

A less-mobile dog needs a routine of regular outdoor visits—he can use these opportunities to help avoid indoor accidents.

Training the
Older Dog

Providing a Change

If your dog can no longer chase after a ball with great speed, he will still enjoy having a toy that needs to be manipulated to obtain a healthy treat hidden inside. Training your dog to play with new toys and participate in new games can provide him with plenty of amusement, although perhaps not for as long as when he was young.

Dogs will continue learning throughout their lives, and mental stimulation is an important aspect of keeping them healthy. Even if your dog hasn't had much training in the past, you can train an old dog to do new tricks—or to respond to a different signal.

Training your dog to do something different or to respond to a new sound can help keep him mentally stimulated. Or you might want to introduce a new signal because your dog doesn't respond to a whistle that he can no longer hear. Establishing new training methods with your dog can also help him to settle into a routine as he becomes older—something that many older dogs cherish.

A Simple Signal

You can start by using a low-pitched bell (a better frequency for an older dog) before your dog does something he enjoys: being fed, having a massage, or being let outdoors. If your dog cannot hear the sound, try stamping your feet—he'll feel the vibrations—or using a flashlight. Once your dog is used to the signal, you can use it, for example, to get him up and about, although he may prefer to stay in bed for a longer nap.

When your dog responds to you and the signal, give him some positive feedback. Praise him, pat him on his head, and give

A flashlight signal helps Rowan, an 8-year-old border collie that has a hearing problem, to understand her owner's commands.

him an occasional reward of a healthy treat, such as a carrot. Keep these sessions short—no longer than 10 minutes—and if you're using them to get the dog to do something more difficult, don't expect miracles.

Starting With an Older Dog

The challenges may be greater if you adopt an older dog (see pages 20–21) from a shelter. Unless the shelter has been looking after the dog for some time, its staff is unlikely to be aware of any behavioral problems. Before deciding to take on such a dog, you need to spend time together, which should include you taking the dog out for walks if possible. This will give you an opportunity to discover how the dog walks when on a leash and whether he has mastered basic commands, such as "sit," and, most important, how he responds to you.

If the dog does not appear to have been trained, don't despair—he can learn. However, you may want to seek professional help by signing up your pet for training classes. In these classes, you will go through the basics and work to correct any individual problems that your pet may have developed, such as repeated barking. It can take longer to train an adult dog than a puppy, so be patient.

Housebreaking an Older Dog

If a new dog has been in kennels for some time, you may need to reeducate him in housebreaking. Always encourage your dog to go outside after meals, as well as first thing in the morning and again last thing at night. This is the best way to prevent accidents in the home, and it helps to establish a routine from the beginning.

Case History

Dylan in Disgrace

Dylan developed the habit of jumping up onto chairs and tables to steal food when his owner wasn't around. His mischievous ways were playing havoc with the family's dinner routine. All dogs will steal food—especially meaty items. A dog's natural pack instincts will make him want to grab what he can before someone else in the pack does! Some dogs, especially hounds, become obese thanks to this instinctive behavior. Fortunately, Dylan isn't overweight. However, now his owner knows she can't leave him alone in the kitchen—his instincts are stronger than his training. Dylan is banned from the kitchen while food is prepared.

Traveling and
Vacations

Wearing a life jacket keeps Mack, a 6-year-old cairn terrier, safe on his owner's boat.

Although life may at times be somewhat fast-paced for an older dog, there is no reason why your pet cannot continue to travel with you when you go on vacation. However, there are times when you'll need to leave your dog at home or in the kennel.

When taking your dog with you on vacation, do not forget to take along his regular medication. You should also pack a few familiar items from home, such as your pet's bed and perhaps a favorite toy. There are a number of hotels that will accept dogs, and you should be able to find these through listings of dog-friendly hotels. Taking your dog with you on vacation will probably be less expensive than booking him into a boarding kennel—and you will not be separated from your pet.

When Your Dog Cannot Vacation

There may be times when alternative arrangements need to be made because dogs are not allowed where you'll be visiting or the traveling would be too strenuous for your dog. The most obvious choice may be to place your dog in a boarding kennel. If your dog has stayed in a boarding kennel in the past, then this is certainly an option, especially if the owners know him. However, they may not be enthusiastic about taking an elderly dog that needs regular medication or that may be displaying behavioral problems. Furthermore, there is no guarantee that just because your dog has been happy in a boarding kennel in the past, he will be happy again if his mental faculties begin to decline and his physical health starts to become poor.

In this situation the best solution is to find a reliable house sitter, who can live in your home while you are away and take care of your dog, giving him any medication as necessary. Be aware, however, that it is

Staying with Relatives

It is sometimes difficult to leave an elderly dog with relatives or friends, even if you have successfully done so when he was younger. This applies particularly if your dog has become restless and does no longer sleep well, or if he has developed incontinence. If you want to stay in close contact with your dog while you are away, the best solution may be to take him with you and to arrange for him to stay at a kennel near you.

important to thoroughly check references. This area of dog care is growing rapidly, partly in response to the growing number of seniors in the canine population. It also provides increased security in your absence.

Before you go, it is important to get your dog accustomed to being cared for by his temporary provider. Arrange an introduction and go out for a walk together. If you have an elderly dog that needs regular injections or pills, it helps to choose a house sitter who has extensive experience with dogs, such as a veterinary nurse. A reliable agency will seek to match up your needs closely with the skills of a suitable sitter. Always give plenty of notice, because during busy periods when many people are on vacation, demand for house sitters increases significantly—just as it does at boarding kennels.

Don't Forget

When you are going away and leaving your dog either at a boarding kennel or in the care of a house sitter, be sure to leave a chart that lists the times when your pet will need to be given his medication. It may help to prepare a day-by-day breakdown, with an accompanying check box, to make it as simple as possible. In case of an emergency, it is important to leave the veterinarian's phone number, along with your contact information.

A travel carrier bag or container designed for dogs are ideal for small dogs, such as Bailey, an 8-year-old Havanese. They are available in different sizes.

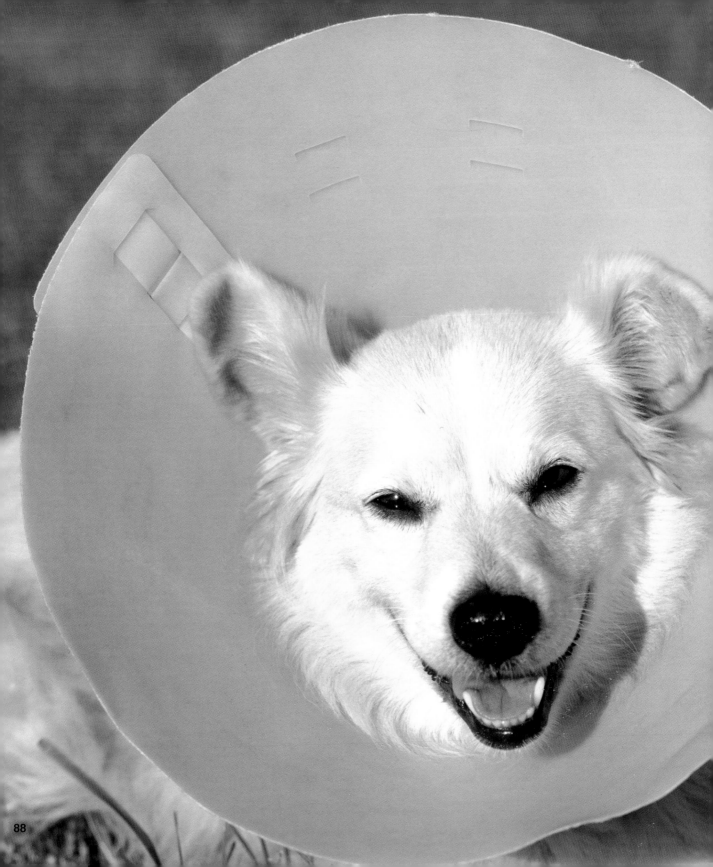

6 Everyday Ailments

As dogs grow older, they are increasingly likely to develop health problems that are linked with the wear on their bodies. Somewhat like the parts of a machine, their organs start to function less effectively with age. Although these changes cannot be reversed, in many cases it is possible to delay the effects of aging. Medical treatments and regular checkups are often vital, but altering your dog's lifestyle and diet can sometimes play a more significant part in your pet's health and well-being during his later years. Your veterinarian will recommend the best approach to keeping your dog healthy and happy.

Urinary Tract

The two kidneys filter the blood to remove waste, but most of the filtered fluid is reabsorbed to conserve water. If too much or too little urine is passing from your dog, or if the urine is discolored, your dog will need veterinary help.

A kidney lies on each side of the dog's body in the abdominal area. Each kidney has 400,000 individual filtration units, called nephrons. They have a semipermeable membrane, which allows molecules to pass through into the renal tubule, but blood cells are normally excluded. Some substances are absorbed back into the body; others pass down through the tubule, ultimately forming urine.

When Things Go Wrong

The ability of the kidneys to filter blood can be affected by problems within the kidneys or the urinary tract, and the first symptoms are often linked to the quantity of urine produced or its frequency. For

Filtered urine passes from the kidneys to the bladder through a pair of ureters. The dog will usually feel the need to pass the urine once the bladder is full. The urine will travel through the urethra, which is longer in a male dog, to leave the body. The prostate gland, which surrounds the urethra just below the bladder, secretes a fluid, which is used for ejaculation in males.

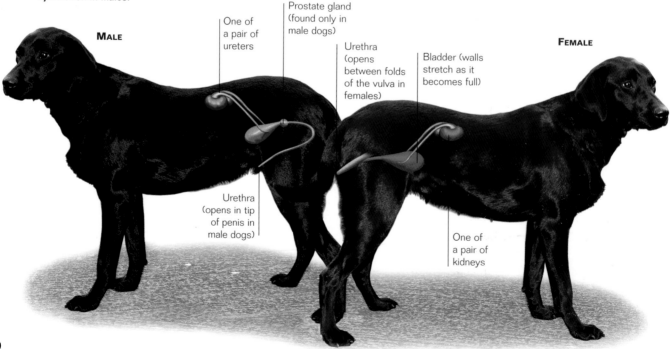

MALE

One of a pair of ureters

Prostate gland (found only in male dogs)

Urethra (opens between folds of the vulva in females)

Bladder (walls stretch as it becomes full)

FEMALE

Urethra (opens in tip of penis in male dogs)

One of a pair of kidneys

example, an antidiuretic hormone (ADH) released from the pituitary gland in the brain acts on the nephrons to increase the uptake of water back into the body if there is a danger of the dog becoming dehydrated, such as during hot weather or periods of decreased drinking. However, if the nephrons become damaged, which occurs if the dog has chronic kidney failure (see pages 94–97), there are insufficient nephrons left to respond to ADH and more water passes out of the body as urine. The dog produces more urine than normal, so he has to drink more to prevent himself from becoming dehydrated.

The Thirsty Dog

Increased thirst in older dogs can also be a symptom of dogs with diabetes mellitus (see pages 134–37) and Cushing's disease (see page 131) and a side effect of certain drugs, such as corticosteroids, which may encourage your pet to drink more than in the past. If you think your dog is drinking more than before, try to quantify this for your veterinarian; for example, use a measuring cup to fill your dog's bowl so you know exactly how much water your dog is drinking.

Urinary tract infections

Older dogs often develop urinary tract infections, which may be linked to other illnesses, such as diabetes mellitus. Dogs will usually produce an acidic urine, which helps to kill potentially harmful microbes. However, in the case of a dog with diabetes mellitus, sugar is lost into the urine and provides an ideal medium for the growth of bacteria.

Female dogs are more susceptible to urinary infections than male dogs because the tube known as the urethra, along which urine flows from the bladder out of the body, is shorter in the female dog. This means that so-called ascending infections, which enter from outside the body, can reach a female dog's bladder more easily.

Treating an Infection

Antibiotic treatment should eliminate the infection. However, there may be an underlying health problem, such as a metabolic condition, that makes your dog more prone to infections and makes relapses common. Urinary tract infections may be linked with uroliths, or stones (also known as calculi; see pages 92–93), and even tumors, so further investigations will be required if antibiotics fail to clear an infection.

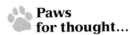

Paws for thought...

Never restrict your dog's access to drinking water, because doing so can endanger your pet's life. If a dog becomes dehydrated, there can be a circulatory collapse, where water is lost from the blood, which then becomes concentrated.

Symptoms of Urinary Tract Infection

- Repeated licking of the urethral opening.

- More frequent urination than normal.

- Discolored urine in some but not all cases.

Prostate problems

The prostate gland, which is present only in male dogs, surrounds the top of the urethra. It normally produces secretions that are added to the dog's sperm. Infection of the prostate is not uncommon in older dogs, especially if the gland becomes enlarged, which frequently occurs in middle-aged male dogs. An infection can be treated with a long course of antibiotics—lasting for up to two months—to eliminate the bacteria.

Enlarged Prostate

In male dogs that are over eight years old, the prostate can become enlarged—the reason for this is unknown, although it may be linked to a hormonal problem. There is also a risk that any swelling may be cancerous. Your veterinarian may need to perform a rectal examination to confirm a diagnosis. If cancer is suspected, further investigation may be necessary. Your veterinarian may perform an ultrasound or take radiographs, which will help to reveal if there are any secondary tumors. For example, the cancer may have spread (known technically as "metastasized") to other organs, such as the liver. In this case the outlook is bleak; otherwise, surgery to remove this gland, although difficult, can be successful.

Other Treatments

Whether or not the prostate gland is swollen or cancerous, castration is also recommended if the procedure was not performed on your dog at an earlier stage in his life. If the gland is simply swollen, your veterinarian may also suggest administering the so-called "female" sex hormone known as estrogen. This treatment will help to shrink the size of the prostate gland.

Acute kidney failure and stones

"Acute" kidney failure means "rapid" kidney failure, and unlike chronic (or long-standing) kidney failure (see pages 94–97), it is an immediate life-threatening condition. It can strike at any age, although it occurs most often in older dogs, and it is often linked with the presence of uroliths, or stones, in the urinary tract. These deposits can occur for several reasons, including an infection or a metabolitic disorder, and they can cause a serious blockage that can obstruct the flow of urine and lead to pressure building up in the

---

Symptoms of an Enlarged Prostate

- Straining noticeably when defecating or urinating.

- Chronic constipation caused by pain when straining to defecate.

Natural Remedies

Adding a little soybean component to your dog's diet, either as a small quantity of powder or as tofu (soybean curd), may provide some protection against further prostate swelling. Genistein, a chemical in soybean, may block the development of prostate cancer.

kidneys. Dehydration, collapse, and rapid death can occur if prompt treatment is not administered. For this reason, it is always important to check that your dog is urinating regularly.

Treating Acute Kidney Failure

Where available, treatment of acute kidney failure may involve hemodialysis, which filters the blood to remove waste from it. However, it is not widely used on dogs with kidney failure, largely because of the cost of the equipment and the difficulty of persuading a dog to sit still long enough to allow the procedure to be performed. The dog will receive fluids and electrolytes to maintain circulation, usually intravenously. Rehydration and treatment of the underlying cause of the problem are essential. Larger stones are often removed by surgery, and the dog may be put on a special diet.

> **Symptoms of Kidney Failure and Stones**
>
> - Crouching position as the dog strains to urinate due to urinary tract pain.
>
> - Extreme straining to urinate but failure to pass urine, which can lead to severe pain and shock.

Case History

Danny the Dalmatian

Danny is a six-year-old dalmatian that suddenly had difficulty urinating, and there was blood in his urine briefly beforehand. The veterinarian suspected that he had kidney stones, known as uroliths or calculi, in his urinary tract. This can be a particular problem in middle-aged male dalmatians because of a metabolic quirk linked to how they break down the chemical purine in their bodies. Danny needed quick treatment using a catheter to clear the blockage and reestablish his urine flow. The stones were made of urate and were small, so X-rays would not detect them. (Phosphate stones are more common in dogs with a chronic urinary tract infection.)

To reduce Danny's risk of developing more kidney stones, he now has a special prescription diet that lessens the risk of a purine buildup, and his owner gives him sodium bicarbonate to keep his urine neutral to slightly alkaline. He is also helped by the drug allopurinol, which reduces the amount of uric acid present in his urine. His owner also makes sure Danny drinks plenty of water.

Chronic kidney failure

It is not always easy to recognize the early symptoms of illnesses associated with aging, because the effects are often insidious and the organs may have what is sometimes referred to as "spare capacity." This certainly applies in cases of chronic kidney failure (also known as chronic renal failure), which affects all older dogs to a greater or lesser extent, as the function of their kidneys declines with age.

The symptoms of chronic kidney failure will not be obvious until approximately three-quarters of the nephrons in the kidneys are lost. Because the kidneys will no longer remove waste matter from the blood efficiently, it will build up and have a toxic effect on the body. Other symptoms may be noticed, too.

Diagnosing Chronic Kidney Failure

One of the ways to check the kidneys' function is to run a complete urine analysis. This test can reveal if substances, such as protein or glucose, are being lost in the urine, which suggests a kidney problem. If you are collecting a sample of your dog's urine to take to your veterinarian, you need to obtain only a small amount of urine. Make sure the sample is fresh, and try to catch the middle part of the urine, known as the "midstream catch," for the best sample. To avoid any risk of contamination, use only a container designed for collecting urine.

Your veterinarian may also want to take a blood sample to obtain an accurate reading of the levels of key metabolites, which are affected by kidney function. The extent to which blood urea nitrogen (sometimes abbreviated BUN) and creatinine are raised will help your veterinarian determine the severity of the problem. Other useful tests include radiography and ultrasound, which provide images of the kidneys that can help detect abnormalities.

Paws for thought...

Always make sure a dog with increased thirst has the opportunity to go outside to urinate more frequently. Otherwise, if the dog has chronic kidney failure, he will likely have accidents in the house.

!

Caution

Dogs normally recover rapidly from vomiting or diarrhea; however, these symptoms are much more serious if your pet has chronic kidney failure, partly because they can alter the fluid balance in the body. This can lead rapidly to dehydration, acute kidney failure, and collapse. Do not delay in seeking veterinary advice.

Dealing with Chronic Kidney Failure

Although there is no actual cure for this illness, it can often be managed successfully, with the dog's condition stabilized for relatively long periods of time and the pet enjoying a good quality of life. However, treatment may be necessary at first, depending on how far the condition has been able to advance in your dog.

Fluid therapy—in which fluids are given by injection subcutaneously (under the skin) in milder cases or by intravenous injection (through a vein) in more serious cases—is often necessary to address the dehydration that is such a prominent feature of chronic kidney failure. The veterinarian can determine which is the best treatment to give from the blood tests. This alone can make a dog much happier and more lively, and it can help to rekindle your pet's appetite, too.

Symptoms of Kidney Failure

Typical indicators associated with kidney failure are:

- Increased thirst—the dog can no longer make concentrated urine due to the damage in his kidneys, so he needs more fluids to make urine.

- Greater urinary output—less water is being reabsorbed by the kidneys.

- More frequent need to urinate—resulting from the increase in urinary flow, which fills the bladder more quickly.

- Noticeably unpleasant breath in advanced cases—caused by the raised concentration of urea in the blood. This causes your dog's breath to have a smell similar to ammonia.

- Dullness and lethargy—due to a buildup of metabolites in the blood, often combined with dehydration. In more serious cases, there may be a loss of appetite and/or vomiting. Impaired secretion of the hormone erythropoietin from the kidney will probably mean there are fewer red blood cells in circulation, resulting in anemia.

- Weight loss—resulting from loss of appetite. However, it is also caused by the loss of nutrients in the urine.

- Sores in the mouth in advanced cases—which may be linked to raised urea and also to water-soluble B vitamins being lost through the kidneys. These are normally reabsorbed, not stored, in the body.

To test for dehydration, pinch a fold of loose skin at the back of the dog's neck. If the dog is healthy, the skin will be elastic and quickly return to its normal shape. If the dog is dehydrated, the skin will take a minute or so to return to its original shape. There will also be signs of pressure marks, because dehydrated skin loses its elasticity.

Natural Remedies

Omega-3 fatty acids are included in some diets for chronic kidney failure because they can lower the blood pressure in the remaining nephrons. This in turn means they are less likely to be damaged and can help to slow down the onset of kidney failure. Omega-3 fatty acids are found in fish oil, derived from tuna, salmon, and other oily fish, and they can be purchased in the form of capsules from many health-food stores.

The importance of special diets

In the longer term your dog will need significant dietary changes to reduce the strain on his kidneys and decrease the harmful waste products building up in his circulation. Several specially formulated commercial diets produced for dogs that have chronic kidney failure are available from veterinarians. These dog foods are designed to help your dog in a number of different ways. For example, their protein content is relatively low but easily assimilated into the body to reduce the burden of nitrogenous waste, and they are supplemented with important water-soluble vitamins and minerals. However, they also differ because some are intended for early stages of the illness, whereas others are designed to help more advanced cases.

The Blood-Pressure Connection

High blood pressure (known as hypertension) affects over half of all dogs with chronic kidney failure, and this may be linked with their inability to control the sodium level in their body effectively because of the decline in kidney function. As a result, special diets for these dogs have much lower sodium levels than those found in ordinary pet foods. The dog's veterinarian may also prescribe medication to reduce and regulate blood pressure.

Calcium and the Kidneys

The kidneys play an important part in maintaining and regulating the body's calcium stores. They activate vitamin D, which stimulates the uptake of calcium from the intestinal tract, and they also break down parathyroid hormone, which triggers the breakdown of calcium in the body, where it is stored in the bones. Excretion of phosphorus is another of the tasks undertaken by the kidneys, and there is a close association between this mineral and calcium.

In cases of kidney damage, there is a risk that not only will calcium not be absorbed properly, but it will also be lost from the body in increasing amounts while phosphorus is retained. Calcium may be deposited in the soft tissues as bone is broken down in excessive amounts due to the influence of circulating parathyroid hormone, with a high level of calcium being carried in the bloodstream. If calcium is deposited in the kidneys, this will compromise their ability to function even further. Therefore, specially formulated foods for dogs with chronic kidney failure are low in phosphorus, helping to maintain a healthy skeletal structure. However, if these foods are not effective, a separate medication may be prescribed to restrict the absorption of phosphorus in the dog's intestinal tract.

The Diet and Protein

Lowering the amount of protein in the diet will reduce the amount of waste products, such as urea, in the blood. However, some dogs with chronic kidney failure actually need more protein to compensate for the protein being lost from the kidneys; otherwise, they will start to lose weight and conditioning. As a compromise, it is important to use protein of so-called "high biological value," which the body can utilize efficiently to minimize the waste matter. Before formulated diets for chronic kidney failure were widely available, hard-boiled eggs were commonly used in homemade diets for this reason.

One of the difficulties is the nausea that often accompanies chronic kidney failure, resulting in the dog not eating with much enthusiasm. Therefore, it is important to find a diet that your dog will eat readily and to monitor his appetite. It may be that a canned diet instead of a dry one will be necessary because canned food is often tastier. If weight loss is a serious issue, then your veterinarian may prescribe anabolic steroids to stimulate your pet's appetite.

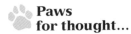

Paws for thought...

A beneficial long-term effect of a special diet for dogs with chronic kidney failure is that it can enhance the activity of the bone marrow, where red blood cells are produced, which helps to prevent anemia.

Frequent urination was the first sign of chronic kidney failure in seven-year-old Bentley. His owner took the dog to the veterinarian, who recommended a change in the dog's diet.

The Digestive System

One of the most significant problems for an older dog starts at the beginning of the digestive system—in the mouth—particularly when a dog's teeth have not been routinely cleaned. However, there are other areas of the digestive tract that change with age, including the muscles that assist the intestines, and these can have an impact on your dog's health.

Inside the mouth

A buildup of plaque affecting the teeth and gums (see pages 28–31) is common, and at least three-quarters of all dogs already have symptoms associated with periodontal disease by the time they are only three years old. A dog that has dental pain will be reluctant to eat properly, and he will be less inclined to play, because picking up

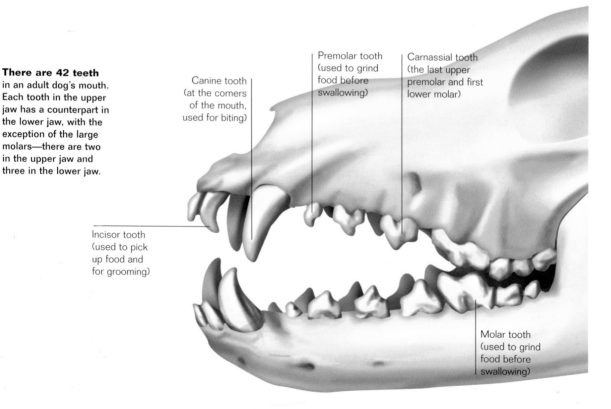

There are 42 teeth in an adult dog's mouth. Each tooth in the upper jaw has a counterpart in the lower jaw, with the exception of the large molars—there are two in the upper jaw and three in the lower jaw.

Canine tooth (at the corners of the mouth, used for biting)

Premolar tooth (used to grind food before swallowing)

Carnassial tooth (the last upper premolar and first lower molar)

Incisor tooth (used to pick up food and for grooming)

Molar tooth (used to grind food before swallowing)

and carrying a toy in his mouth will be painful. By this stage a tooth will often become loose in the mouth and will need to be removed under anesthesia.

Your veterinarian may take a few dental X-rays, which will show the amount of damage that has occurred below the gum line, particularly before he cleans the teeth. Otherwise, once the plaque has been stripped off, the tooth may be so loose that it virtually falls out because it may have been held in place only by the plaque surrounding its base. Antibiotics are usually prescribed after dental extractions to prevent an infection from entering the bloodstream and spreading to the vital organs.

A Broken Tooth

Your dog will use its teeth to chew and gnaw, and he is at risk of breaking a tooth if he tries to bite something that is harder than his teeth, such as a stone picked up on a beach. It is often one of the long, pointed canine teeth at the corner of the mouth that is damaged in this way. This injury may not be immediately noticeable, but it can be painful at times. If you watch your dog eating, you may notice that he tries to avoid using the side of his mouth that has the damaged tooth. The situation can become worse even if the dog is not showing great signs of discomfort, because the break will enable infection to gain access to the interior of the tooth more easily. An infected tooth will need a root canal or should be removed.

Dental Changes

Although a dog can adapt well to losing some of his long, pointed canines, they are important to help keep his tongue correctly positioned in his mouth, preventing it from lolling outside his jaws. Further back, lying just below the front of the eye sockets, the large carnassial teeth also play a particularly significant role. These large teeth have a shearing action that will cut their way through pieces of food that are too large for the dog to swallow whole. If your dog has lost most of the molars at the back of his mouth, you may need to cut up his food into smaller pieces, particularly when you are offering him fresh foods, such as cooked meats.

Swollen Gums

If the gum margins become persistently traumatized by the presence of tartar, this may trigger an overgrowth of gum tissue, causing what are known as epulides. These are most common in older dogs, particularly in breeds with compact, rounded faces, such as boxers. Unfortunately, food and other debris may become trapped in these swollen areas, so they may need to be trimmed away surgically.

Symptoms of Dental Problems

- Your dog drops some of its food with increasing frequency. This is an indicator of dental pain, not loss of coordination.

- Your dog develops bad breath. Although this can be linked with more generalized health problems, such as chronic kidney failure (see pages 94–97), it is a common symptom of a dental problem.

- Your dog eats with an unusually tilted head. This is an indication that there is pain on one side of the mouth, which may be caused by a tooth or gum problem.

After food is swallowed, it reaches the stomach via the esophagus, or gullet. The food is broken down in the stomach's acid environment before it passes on to the intestinal tract. The digestion of food occurs in the small intestine as enzymes split the chemical components of the food, which enter the body through the intestinal wall. Undigested material continues into the large intestine, where water may be absorbed, before passing out of the body as feces.

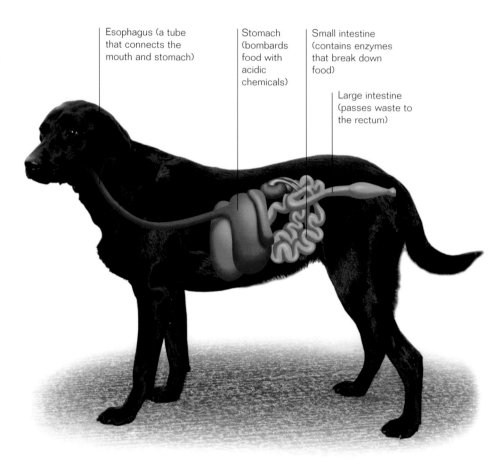

Esophagus (a tube that connects the mouth and stomach)

Stomach (bombards food with acidic chemicals)

Small intestine (contains enzymes that break down food)

Large intestine (passes waste to the rectum)

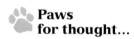

Paws for thought...

It is common for a dog to briefly have diarrhea after being constipated. The cause is simply that the rhythm of the gut has been disturbed and needs time to settle down again.

Esophagus

In older dogs the esophagus can become wider than normal and lose its ability to push food along its path. The cause of this condition, known as acquired idiopathic megaesophagus, is unclear, and its treatment is difficult. There is a risk that food may enter the windpipe instead of the esophagus because its entrance is also at the back of the mouth, and this can lead to pneumonia. Your veterinarian can check your dog's esophagus by using a viewing tube known as an endoscope to determine if your dog has this illness.

Intestinal problems

Constipation is the most common problem that affects an older dog's digestive system. It can be due to a loss of muscle tone, which makes it hard for the dog to force out his feces. The situation will be worse if your dog also has arthritis in his hips. The straining will be painful, so your dog will be more reluctant to relieve himself. The feces will accumulate, and as it loses water in the colon, it will become harder, which will cause further discomfort. In cold weather an older dog can be more susceptible to constipation, because he does not want to venture outside into the cold.

A laxative or, in a severe case, an enema may be given by your veterinarian. If you are feeding your dog wet food, you can add bran fiber to increase bulk, and a little canned pumpkin can be useful as a laxative. If your dog has dry food, switch him to a senior formula, which has extra fiber to help prevent constipation.

Other Causes of Constipation

A perineal hernia can occur in an older, unneutered male dog. The hormone testosterone weakens the surrounding muscles at the end of the intestinal tract, causing the intestinal tract to bulge out and create depressions where fecal matter can become trapped. An affected dog will pass feces, but he continues to strain because he cannot force the trapped material out of his body. He will need surgery to repair the weakness in the muscle wall.

Liver problems

As a dog ages, he becomes more vulnerable to liver problems. This organ is a detoxifying center in the body, especially for drugs, and receives blood containing nutrients from the small intestine. A problem can affect the liver's ability to perform these functions. Symptoms of liver ailments are often vague at first, but an enlarged liver, often detected by your veterinarian as part of a routine examination, is a cause for concern, which can be investigated further by blood tests.

A number of breeds—especially the Doberman, Bedlington terrier, West Highland terrier, and Skye terrier—are vulnerable to a buildup of copper in the liver tissue, which can trigger chronic hepatitis, particularly after they reach middle age. Normally, copper flows along the bile duct into the part of the small intestine known as the duodenum, where it is excreted in bile. Copper-storage disease is treated with a special low-copper diet.

Vomiting and Diarrhea

It is normal for dogs to have occasional episodes of vomiting and diarrhea, often because they have been scavenging. However, in older dogs these symptoms can have a more serious cause and may indicate a potentially life-threatening illness. It is particularly important to seek veterinary advice if your pet is known to have chronic kidney disease or heart failure, because the dog's treatment may need to be changed.

Tumor Risk

Within the colon, just as in other parts of the digestive tract, the risk of tumors increases with age, and sometimes a tumor in the colon causes constipation. By this stage a dog will show more generalized symptoms of ill-health. The tumor is likely to be cancerous, but it may be removed by surgery if the cancer is not advanced.

Heart Ailments

Symptoms of CHF

- Fatigue.

- Coughing.

- Breathlessness.

- Slight blueness in the area around the lips and inside the mouth.

- Lying with the elbows held out from the body.

- Fainting.

- Neck held extended to aid breathing.

The heart is responsible for pumping blood around the body. It is essential that the heart beats rhythmically if it is to work efficiently without affecting the dog's health.

A rhythmical heartbeat is achieved by electrical impulses, which are generated by special pacemaker cells in the heart. The heartbeats echo throughout the arterial system, and they can be felt at various points on the dog's body, just under the skin, creating what is known as the pulse. It can usually be detected in the femoral artery, at the top of the dog's hind leg. A dog's pulse is typically between 75 and 120 beats per minute, depending on the patient's size. Small dogs have a faster heart rate; large dogs, a slower one.

Congestive heart failure (CHF)

Just as with any pump, the dog's heart is likely to work less efficiently as he becomes older, often because the mitral and tricuspid valves,

Blood from the body enters the heart, which has four chambers, and empties into the chamber known as the right atrium. It passes into the right ventricle, which pumps it to the lungs. After being reoxygenated in the lungs, the blood returns to the left atrium before being pumped out into the aorta from the left ventricle. The blood then disperses around the body through progressively smaller blood vessels.

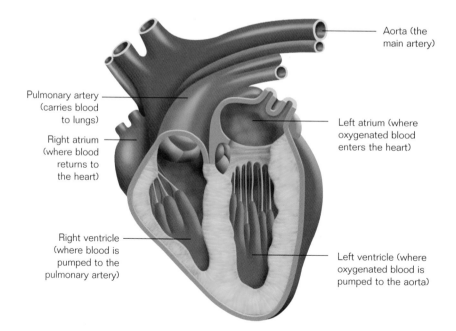

Aorta (the main artery)

Pulmonary artery (carries blood to lungs)

Right atrium (where blood returns to the heart)

Left atrium (where oxygenated blood enters the heart)

Right ventricle (where blood is pumped to the pulmonary artery)

Left ventricle (where oxygenated blood is pumped to the aorta)

which separate the atrium and ventricle on the left and right side respectively, start to leak. This will ultimately lead to the condition known as congestive heart failure (CHF), although the specific symptoms will be influenced by whether just one or both of these valves are affected.

When the mitral valve fails to form a tight seal, there is a backflow of blood from the left ventricle back into the atrium. This has two effects. First, the atrium becomes abnormally enlarged, and it then exerts pressure on the adjacent windpipe, which usually causes coughing, particularly at night. Second, the amount of blood being pumped out of the ventricle at each contraction is also reduced. This causes fluid buildup in the lungs, known as pulmonary edema, which leads to a cough and eventually more severe respiratory dificulties.

If the tricuspid valve is affected, this creates back pressure, which will slow down the return of blood to the heart. This will soon result in a buildup of fluid in the abdominal cavity, known as ascites, which is an indication of right-sided heart failure. Known as chronic valvular endocardiosis, this illness is the most common cause of chronic heart failure and is usually seen in smaller breeds, especially Cavalier King Charles spaniels.

Dilated cardiomyopathy

A cardiac problem that tends to affect larger breeds is dilated cardiomyopathy, but the condition can also develop in cocker spaniels. The cause of this illness lies in the ventricles, which do not contract normally, resulting in a reduced output of blood from the heart. In some cases a dog can die suddenly without previously showing any symptoms from this illness. However, it is more usual for an affected individual to have progressive signs of chronic heart failure.

The symptoms differ, depending on whether one or both ventricles are affected. If left untreated, the ventricles become so dilated that they can no longer pump effectively and lose their muscle tone, and their muscular walls become thinner as a result. Ultimately, the valves separating the ventricles from the atria will also start to leak as the ventricles become engorged with blood, and the resulting pressure in these chambers causes a backflow of blood.

Distinguishing Heart Failure

Left Side
Difficulty in breathing as fluid builds up in the lungs.

Right Side
Fluid collects in the abdomen, which causes swelling in the lower part of the limbs.

Breeds Susceptible to Dilated Cardiomyopathy

- Great Dane (below)
- Doberman
- Irish wolfhound
- Cocker spaniel

An inside view of the heart and its chambers can be taken with an ultrasound.

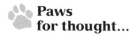 **Paws for thought...**

Blood tests may be helpful for older dogs that have a heart ailment, because they provide insight into how other organs, such as the kidneys, may have been affected.

Nutritional Links

The cause of dilated cardiomyopathy is unclear, although it has been discovered that certain key nutrients may sometimes be deficient in the diets of affected dogs. In the case of cocker spaniels, the amino acid taurine, which is a vital dietary component, has been implicated. This amino acid is routinely supplemented in cat food, because cats cannot manufacture it. However, the vast majority of dogs can obtain taurine from their food naturally, so it is not usually added as a separate ingredient to their diets. A supplement may be necessary.

Diagnosing heart failure

If your dog is suspected of having heart failure, there are a number of ways in which your veterinarian will be able to investigate and assess your dog's condition. The methods used will depend somewhat on what the veterinarian believes is the cause of the underlying problem.

The most obvious diagnostic method is for your veterinarian to listen to the dog's heart using a stethoscope. A dog's heart lies in the left-hand side of the chest cavity, roughly in the position where the point of the flexed elbow lies across the chest. The veterinarian will be specifically listening for a sound known as a murmur, which is caused if there is a seepage of blood resulting from a valvular problem within the organ.

Picturing the Heart

Taking X-ray pictures of the heart, known as radiographs, can also be useful in assessing the state of your dog's condition. These pictures can provide information on the overall size of the heart and which areas may be enlarged, as well as any other associated problems in the chest, including any changes that occur in the lungs.

One way to get an internal view of the chambers of the heart is by using ultrasound to create what is known as an echocardiogram. With this image it is possible to see the internal contractions of the chambers and to visualize how the valves are working. Your veterinarian will be able to see any abnormalities that may be present. This technique is easy to perform and won't cause your dog discomfort. An echocardiogram is also useful for monitoring a dog once he starts medication to determine how his condition is responding to treatment.

Your veterinarian can also perform a specific examination of the electrical rhythm of the heart by using an electrocardiogram, which provides a trace of the underlying electrical muscle activity. This can highlight problems with the heartbeat itself, as well as with the valves in the heart.

Once your veterinarian has performed these tests, he will know why your dog's heart is not functioning properly and will be able to recommend the most appropriate treatment.

> **Blood Pressure and Dogs**
>
> Blood pressure measurements are less commonly used for dogs than people because of the wide variations in blood pressure that exist between different breeds. It can be difficult to obtain a resting baseline, especially because dogs are not relaxed in a veterinary consulting room.
>
> There is also the difficulty in where to place the cuff—it is usually wrapped around the tail to take the reading. Blood pressure is measured in millimeters of mercury, and the first, higher reading is taken at systole, when the ventricles are forcing the blood through the heart. The second, lower diastolic figure is noted when the heart is refilling, and the pressure should be significantly lower.

A heart murmur can be detected by listening to a dog's heart through a stethoscope.

Caution
If your dog has bad teeth, bacteria can spread from them via the blood to the heart, which can trigger a valvular infection. By keeping your dog's teeth in good condition (see pages 28–31), you will help guard against the risk of heart disease.

Treating heart disease

As more blood is retained in the heart and not pushed out into the body, fluid builds up in the circulation. The kidneys will work less effectively because they are receiving the blood that they filter at lower pressure. Treatment is aimed at reducing these symptoms to stabilize the dog's condition—medical treatment will not cure the problem. Drugs known as diuretics, such as frusemide, will be prescribed to reduce the retained fluid and salt. ACE inhibitors may also be recommended to lessen the pressure on the heart and help it function more effectively.

ACE Inhibitors

In a dog that has CHF, the peripheral circulation will shut down to a degree, and the blood vessels will become constricted as a result of the decreased flow of blood from the heart. Along with diuretics, drugs in the ACE inhibitor group are often prescribed. ACE is an abbreviation for angiotensin-converting enzyme. This enzyme normally converts the angiotensin I protein in the blood to the active form, known as angiotensin II, which causes the blood vessels to constrict and raise the blood pressure. An ACE inhibitor blocks this process, which keeps the blood pressure down. It also reduces the work that the heart needs to do because it allows blood to flow through the vessels with lower resistance, so less effort will be required to pump it through the body.

Research has shown that when the mitral valve is affected, an ACE inhibitor can double a dog's life expectancy and help to maintain the dog's quality of life. The combination of a diuretic with an ACE inhibitor usually provides good results, although there are other types of medication that can be used, too.

Heartworm and the Heart

In warmer regions where heartworm (*Dirofilaria immitis*) is a problem, continue to routinely give your older dog the medicine recommended by the veterinarian. Otherwise, your pet can still acquire heartworm from a bite by a mosquito carrying it. The tiny larvae will develop in the heart, reaching the size of earthworms and blocking the right side of the heart, which causes heart failure. The worms can be detected by an echocardiogram.

Dietary and Lifestyle Changes

Aside from providing your dog with his regular medication, be prepared to make changes to his diet, too. A low-salt (or low-sodium) diet is recommended, and there are specific prescription diets available that can benefit dogs that have heart ailments.

The use of some supplements might be helpful, but discuss these with your veterinarian before giving them to your dog. An omega-3 fatty-acid supplement may be recommended for the heart. If there is a specific underlying deficiency, such as taurine in a cocker spaniel, your veterinarian may suggest a supplement.

Once your dog displays signs of CHF, you will need to reduce the amount of exercise that he receives. Concentrate on gentle walks instead of demanding hikes. When exercising your dog outdoors, keep him on a leash at first to prevent him from overexerting himself once the medication improves his condition.

Signs of more energy, such as your dog enjoying a walk, is a good indication that treatment for his heart condition is working.

Valvular Surgery

Treatment of valvular disease in older dogs has relied on drugs in the past, but pioneering surgery is now being carried out in this field. The emphasis of this open-heart surgery is based on repairing the valves, not replacing them. Artificial valves are being developed, but a major problem has been the formation of blood clots in the valves, preventing them from working effectively for long. Dogs that have undergone this type of open-heart surgery have subsequently needed anticoagulant drugs to reduce this risk for the rest of their lives.

A pacemaker is implanted under the dog's skin and wired to the heart to keep the beat consistent.

Pacemakers

If there are disturbances in the electrical rhythm of the heart that cannot be corrected by medication, it may be necessary to fit a pacemaker to regulate the rhythm. The use of pacemakers in dogs has advanced since they were first used in the 1980s. This device can detect when the heartbeat is slowing; once it falls to a predetermined level, the pacemaker is activated. The pacemaker unit is implanted beneath the dog's skin.

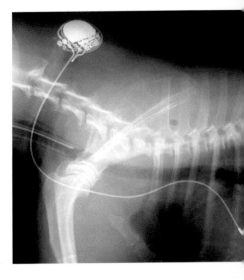

If your dog is fitted with a pacemaker, you will need to check his heart rate regularly to make sure that it is working well. Your veterinarian will show you how to check the heart rate by checking the pulse. Typically, there should be 70–120 beats per minute, depending on the breed and your dog's level of activity. Take the pulse only when your dog has been resting, not after he has been running or had other exercise.

Respiratory System

The respiratory system provides oxygen, which is carried around the dog's body by red blood cells to be used by the body's tissues. It also allows carbon dioxide to diffuse out from the blood when it returns to the lungs so that this gas can be exhaled from the body.

The respiratory system of the dog is controlled by part of the brain known as the respiratory center, which is located in the medulla. It responds to raised levels of carbon dioxide in the blood by sending out nerve impulses, which cause the dog to breathe faster, thus speeding up the interchange with oxygen that occurs in the lungs. Most dogs have a normal respiratory rate of 10–30 breaths per minute, with bigger dogs breathing more slowly than smaller ones.

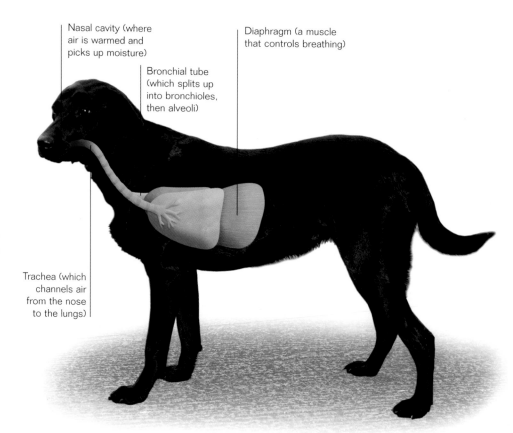

Nasal cavity (where air is warmed and picks up moisture)

Bronchial tube (which splits up into bronchioles, then alveoli)

Diaphragm (a muscle that controls breathing)

Trachea (which channels air from the nose to the lungs)

Air passes into the body through the nasal cavities and flows down the larynx—where the dog's vocal chords are located—into the trachea, or windpipe. The trachea divides into a pair of tubes called bronchi, which enter each lung. The bronchi split up into bronchioles and then into millions of tiny alveoli, where they link with blood vessels and where gaseous exchange takes place.

Laryngeal Paralysis

Breeds susceptible to laryngeal paralysis include the Labrador retriever, bull terrier, dalmatian, Siberian husky, and Bouvier des Flandres. With age a dog's bark may change and fade, and there may be wheezing when breathing in and coughing. These signs are linked to degenerative changes in the larynx. The condition can be confirmed by an endoscopic examination. There is no treatment, but exercise your dog more gently if he has laryngeal paralysis, and offer easy-to-swallow food to lessen the chances of food entering the lungs, where it can cause pneumonia. There is a risk of swelling of the laryngeal tissue, known as edema, which can restrict the airflow into the lungs. It requires emergency treatment.

This flat-faced dog had signs of respiratory distress during Hurricane Katrina.

Tracheal Collapse

The trachea is normally a rigid tube, but in older dogs, particularly small breeds, it may lose its structural strength, which will reduce the flow of air. Careful management, such as keeping your pet free from stress, may help, as will treating any cough. In some cases surgery is the best solution, although there may not be a complete recovery.

Pneumonia

As a dog grows older, the lungs lose their elasticity and work less efficiently. The so-called mucociliary escalator—a protective covering of mucus in the airways that carries tiny inhaled particles of dirt and microbes out of the lungs—also becomes less effective, leaving the dog at risk of developing infections in the airways, such as pneumonia. Cases of pneumonia require rapid treatment. Diagnosis can be made by examining X-rays of the chest. Antibiotics are usually prescribed. Physiotherapy can be beneficial by causing the dog to cough more, which helps to clear the airways so he can breathe more easily.

Symptoms of Pneumonia

- Cough.

- Raised temperature.

- Mucoid discharge from the nose.

- Loss of appetite.

- Lethargic behavior.

Chronic Bronchial Disease

A cough lasting for more than two months is the main symptom of this illness, which tends to afflict smaller dogs over eight years old, especially Yorkshire terriers, Pekingese, Shetland sheepdogs, and Chihuahuas. The underlying cause is unclear, but the problem results from a buildup of mucus in the airways. Steroids and bronchodilators to open the airways can help, as may a specific cough medicine.

Musculoskeletal System

The muscles attached to the dog's skeleton provide the power so that your pet can walk, run, jump, and swim. As a dog grows older, these muscles are at a greater risk of being strained, and the bones are subjected to wear and tear.

Paws for thought...
If your dog is having difficulty walking, it may not be a muscular injury. Check your dog's nails. Particularly in older dogs that have less exercise, these can become overgrown and will need regular trimming (see pages 36–37).

A damaged meniscus pad can deteriorate, causing an inflamed joint. The ligaments that support the joints can become sprained, and the tendons, which attach the muscles to the bones, may be damaged, too. The ligaments and tendons can tear, particularly in obese dogs, because moving the dog's extra weight demands greater effort.

Strains and sprains

The most obvious sign of a strain or sprain is if your dog starts to limp. This often occurs when out for a walk or after your dog has been running. It is important for an older dog that is limping

At 319 bones, a dog's skeleton has roughly 100 more bones than a human skeleton. The size and shape of the bones vary, depending on the breed. When two bones meet, they form a joint, and some joints have a pad of cartilage, known as a meniscus, between the bones that acts as a cushion.

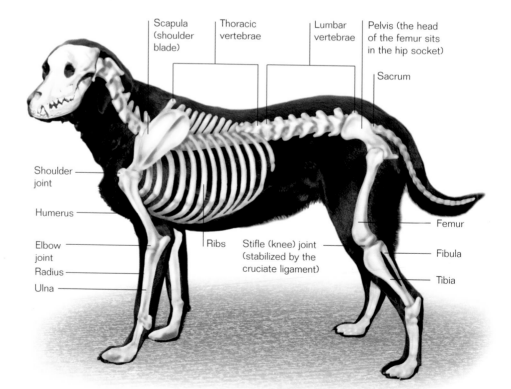

Scapula (shoulder blade)

Thoracic vertebrae

Lumbar vertebrae

Pelvis (the head of the femur sits in the hip socket)

Sacrum

Shoulder joint

Humerus

Elbow joint

Radius

Ulna

Ribs

Stifle (knee) joint (stabilized by the cruciate ligament)

Femur

Fibula

Tibia

Caution

If your dog has had joint or musculoskeletal problems in the past, instead of throwing a ball or other toy for him to chase, take your dog out for progressively longer walks as a way to improve his level of fitness. Otherwise, there is a risk that he may turn awkwardly or stumble and hurt himself.

After a warm-up with her owner, eight-year-old Princess enjoys running after her favorite toy.

to be examined by his veterinarian to determine the cause of the problem and provide the most effective method of treatment. Early intervention from your veterinarian will hopefully prevent any long-term disability from developing.

Prevent Injuries

You can help to prevent these injuries by encouraging your dog to walk on a leash with you for a short time before letting him off so he can run. This will allow him to warm up his muscles. It is also a good idea to ensure your pet wears a coat (see pages 32–33), particularly if he has thin fur, to keep his muscles warm. Muscles that are warm are less likely to be strained.

Weight and the Joints

One of the most harmful conditions to affect the joints is obesity (see pages 50–51). It can place serious, even damaging, strain on the joints, and if your dog has arthritis, obesity can make it a more painful problem. If you cannot feel your dog's ribs, then your dog is probably overweight (see pages 48–49) and needs to lose weight. This can be confirmed by your veterinarian, who will also check your dog's overall state of health. He will help you devise a weight-loss plan for your dog (see pages 52–53), which may include special prescription diet foods and exercise.

Natural Remedies

If your dog needs medication to relieve pain, you could consider acupuncture. It can help an older dog, whether used in conjunction with painkillers or on its own.

Acupuncture can provide pain relief in an older dog that is more tolerant of such treatments than a younger, often more nervous dog.

Hip dysplasia

The hip joints are essential mechanisms in a dog's movement. They transmit the power from the well-muscled hind legs, helping the dog to run fast. These limbs are attached to the hips by ball-and-socket joints. A protuberant ball-like head on the femur at the top of the hind leg fits into the cup-shaped acetabulum on the pelvis.

Particularly in larger dogs, especially German shepherds, the acetabulum can be too shallow and the ball does not fit properly into it, resulting in hind-leg weakness. This condition is known as hip dysplasia, and although there are now programs that monitor the breeding of dogs carefully, the condition still arises regularly. It is a lifelong weakness that cannot be simply corrected.

Not only does hip dysplasia affect the dog's limbs, but it also causes abnormal strains on the hip joint itself. Degenerative changes in the joints often occur in old age and cause pain. Known as osteoarthritis, it is the result of wear on the cartilage protecting the bones, which becomes eroded and results in inflammation.

What Can Be Done?

X-ray pictures should show the severity of the resulting inflammation of the bones. Nonsteroidal anti-inflammatory painkillers may be prescribed by the veterinarian, and supplements, such as glucosamine (see pages 26–27), may also be recommended to help protect the cartilage covering the joint.

If your dog is overweight, it will also be important to help him lose the extra bulk (see pages 52–53) because obesity will worsen the symptoms. Exercise in moderation is also important. It will help build up the muscles, which will ease the pain on the joint. Hydrotherapy (see pages 62–63) is a good option because it will allow your pet to exercise without pain. You may also want to switch your

Case History

Sheba's New Hip

Severe hip dysplasia led to Sheba, a German shepherd, undergoing a hip replacement. However, her hind-leg muscles had wasted away. Known as muscle atrophy, this process is not an actual illness but occurred because Sheba had not been using her hind-leg muscles due to her disability. As a result, the muscles lost their mass and tone. Once Sheba recovered from her surgery, she was put on an exercise plan that included physiotherapy (see pages 72–73), which gradually helped her to build up her muscles. They now have bulk and have become stronger, and Sheba once more can enjoy walks with her owner.

dog to a food that contains chondroprotectants. There is now increasing evidence that these should be incorporated in a dog's diet from an early stage in life for maximum benefit.

Hip Replacements

Surgery to replace the hip joint has become routine in people, and although expensive, it is possible for similar surgery to be performed in an older dog. Replacement hips are available in a range of different sizes. The surgery entails cutting off the end of the femur and drilling out an area so that the base of the titanium replacement hip, complete with its ball head, can be fitted securely into the bone. The acetabulum on the pelvis is replaced with a plastic cup, into which the new head of the femur will be fitted.

After surgery, it will take about two months for a dog to recover fully, and exercise will be initially confined to walking your dog on a leash. Once your dog realizes that the pain is gone, he will soon start to become more active. However, it is important that he does not overexert himself until the joint has had time to become embedded in place. Keep your dog on a leash and prevent him from jumping up.

 Paws for thought...

Although both hips may be causing problems, a dog may need only one hip replacement because he can transfer his weight to the new joint.

Symptoms of Hip Disease

- Your dog has difficulty standing up.

- He appears stiff when starting to walk.

- He may limp after a walk.

- He is reluctant to scratch himself with his hind legs.

- Muscle wasting may be evident around the joints.

- Even a placid dog may snap when picked up, because of the underlying joint pain.

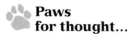

Paws for thought...

Polysulfated glycosaminoglycan (PSGAG), a drug first developed for treating joint damage in horses, can be given by injection to dogs. It may bring relatively fast relief in severe cases, with a distinct improvement after several injections. However, a number of dogs fail to respond to this treatment.

Arthritis

When the cartilage in a joint becomes eroded and inflamed from wear and tear with age, it is known as arthritis. Although the hips are the most commonly affected joints, the elbows and knees may also develop arthritis. Arthritic joints can be painful, but it can be difficult to determine when a dog has painful joints, because he will not yelp unless handled—the pain is chronic instead of a sharp, stabbing pain—and the signs of this problem may be missed earlier in life.

If the cruciate ligament in the knee has been damaged in the past, often because of obesity (see pages 50–51), arthritis often develops in the joint as the dog ages. Unless your dog's weight is reduced, the ligament can rupture, which will necessitate surgical repair.

Treatment for arthritic joint problems is similar to treatment for hip dysplasia (see pages 112–13). Helping an overweight dog lose weight is important, coupled with slow but regular exercise. The impact on the joints will be lessened if your dog walks rather than runs.

Monitoring

When prescribing long-term medication for joint pain—such as nonsteroidal anti-inflammatory drugs to reduce the underlying inflammation and lessen the pain—your veterinarian will want to check that your dog is not experiencing any side effects from it, so blood tests will be required. Some drugs may adversely affect liver function, while aspirin-type medication can predispose your dog to stomach ulcers. Test results suggest that some human

When having an X-ray, it is important for your dog to remain still. He may need to be sedated for this reason.

medications prescribed for arthritis have a lower risk of causing these adverse side effects in dogs and can be just as effective, although they may not be officially approved for this purpose. Your veterinarian can prescribe these—don't give your dog pills prescribed for a family member that have not been prescribed for him.

A Warm Dog Is a Happy Dog

Keeping your dog in warm surroundings will help to offset many of the worst effects of stiffness and joint pain. You can purchase special heating pads that can be warmed in a microwave oven to place in his bed. Grooming your pet after a walk may also be beneficial. Dry him gently with a towel if he is wet to reduce the chances of him becoming cold. Alternatively, if your dog is not disturbed by the noise, you can use a hair dryer on a medium heat setting, but avoid sensitive areas, such as the eyes. A hair dryer may also help to warm up the muscles after a walk on a cold, wet day.

Skeletal changes

It is not just the joints that can be affected by age, but the skeleton as well. Bone is constantly being broken down, replaced, and remodeled throughout a dog's life, and in some cases things can go awry. Metabolic bone disease can be linked with chronic kidney failure (see pages 94–97), where bone is destroyed and not replaced, while the level of calcium in the blood rises.

Another condition of this type is known as spondylosis deformans, which affects larger breeds, such as German shepherd dogs. In this case abnormal bony growths start to develop on the spinal column, particularly in the lumbar vertebrae area. They may go undetected until the bony spurs start to exert pressure on the spinal nerves as they pass from the spinal cord out of the vertebral column. The result is a varying degree of hind-leg weakness, which can lead to paralysis in some instances.

X-ray pictures of the lumbar vertebrae area will reveal the cause of the problem, which can be suggestive of hip dysplasia at first. It is not possible to treat the condition successfully, but anti-inflammatory treatments may provide some relief.

Pain in the Neck

If your dog has a painful neck, you can provide him with raised food bowls so that he will not have to bend his neck to eat. However, in the case of larger breeds or those with a narrow chest, these bowls should be avoided. These breeds are susceptible to bloat, and when feeding from a raised bowl they may ingest air, which will cause the stomach to swell up. Bloat can be a potentially fatal condition, and it is the reason why dogs should be fed only after exercise, not beforehand.

Certain breeds, including the boxer, may develop spondylosis deformans, a type of bone disease.

Muscle-loss problems

Changes that occur within the skeletal structure of the body can be an underlying cause of muscle wasting; however, muscle wasting can also be a normal part of the aging process, reflecting the dog's declining level of activity. In fact, many elderly dogs show signs of muscle loss on the head above the eyes as a result of advancing years. In addition, there are also some specific medical conditions that can result in muscle weakness.

Degenerative Myelopathy

In certain cases what appears to be a muscular problem may lie within the nerves of the muscle instead of in the muscles. In old age some breeds of dog—particularly Welsh corgis and German shepherds—are at risk of developing degenerative myelopathy. One of the effects of this disorder is to cause the outer covering of the nerve fibers, known as myelin, to break down, which prevents the electrical nerve impulses from traveling normally along the nerve fibers. As a result, the skeletal muscles that usually move in response to these nerve impulses become paralyzed. Because they are not moving as they used to, the muscles start to lose their tone and begin to waste away.

Depending on the original source of the problem, the dog is likely to have difficulty moving, and the owner may notice that he often drags his hind feet. The veterinarian can test the dog's reflexes. If the dog has this condition, his reflexes will have mostly disappeared.

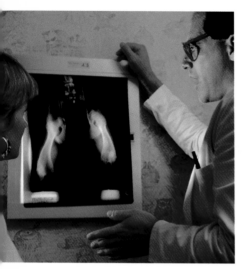

Degenerative problems of the musculosketal system can be diagnosed with the aid of an X-ray. These problems include hip dysplasia and lumbosacral stenosis.

A cart with wheels will allow a dog with hind-leg problems to maintain mobility in his front legs and upper body.

Because there is no available cure for degenerative myelopathy, treatment is essentially based on easing the symptoms. Unfortunately, the condition will continue to worsen until the dog finally loses the use of his hind limbs and becomes paralyzed.

However, just because a dog loses the use of his hind limbs, it does not mean that he cannot carry on living a happy, active life, thanks to the development of special carts with wheels designed to help keep a dog mobile. The dog is strapped to the cart with a harness, and the cart supports the weight of the paralyzed part of the dog. The carts are manufactured in various sizes to suit different breeds. There are even carts designed for quadriplegic dogs that cannot walk at all.

Degenerative Lumbosacral Stenosis

The German shepherd is also the breed that is most commonly affected by an internal narrowing of the vertebrae in the lumbar and sacral region at the end of the spinal column, which is where the tail starts. This condition develops in an older dog, and it constricts the nerves that leave the spinal cord in the region, which interferes with the function of those nerves. Weakness of the hind limbs is a characteristic feature, often combined with incontinence. An affected dog is also likely to have difficulty in wagging his tail.

An X-ray of your dog will help your veterinarian diagnose the condition, but other imaging techniques, such as computed tomography—which provides a sequential cross-sectional view of the bones—will allow him to observe the extent of the problem. It is often possible to operate on the dog and open up the canal. This will free the pressure on the nerves, so that hopefully the symptoms will subsequently disappear.

Unfortunately, the one symptom of this condtion that is most likely not to be resolved by the surgery is urinary incontinence. If your dog is having frequent accidents, you may need a supply of diapers designed for dogs (see pages 82–83).

Is It Bad Luck?

A number of musculoskeletal illnesses occur in German shepherds; however, this does not mean that most or all German shepherds will develop such diseases. Instead, it reflects the fact that this breed is especially popular among dog owners and, therefore, more numerous among the canine population when compared with other types of dog. This also means that there has been a greater opportunity to observe and study such conditions in this breed.

The Brain and Nervous System

The dog's brain and central nervous system coordinates his behavior and responses, with different areas of the brain acting at conscious and involuntary levels. Various problems can plague the system, depending on where it is damaged.

The cerebrum in the upper part of the brain controls the dog's awareness of his environment and what he has learned, interpreting the world around him and reacting to information from his senses. Further back, the hypothalamus acts on the pituitary gland to regulate the dog's internal body activities. The area that controls the dog's movements is known as the cerebellum, which responds to sensors in the body.

The brain stem connects the brain to the spinal cord, forming the central nervous system. This system carries out subconscious functions, such as regulating the heartbeat and the rate of breathing. It also reacts when pain occurs—for example, it causes muscles to contract to pull a limb away from heat or another source of pain.

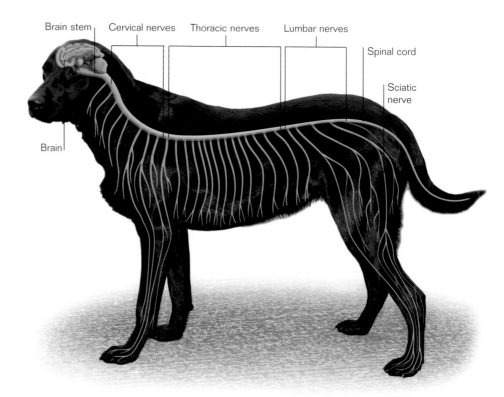

Brain stem | Cervical nerves | Thoracic nerves | Lumbar nerves | Spinal cord | Sciatic nerve | Brain

A harness is a safer option for walking dogs that are prone to disk problems, because they are less likely to cause an injury than attaching a leash to a collar around the neck.

The brain is protected by the skull and the spinal cord running along the back by the vertebral column. The brain and spinal cord are surrounded by the meninges, which protects against trauma; further safeguards in the brain are provided by the fluid-filled ventricles.

Prolapsed disks

A common problem is damage to one or more intervertebral disks, which separate the vertebrae in the spinal cord. These shock absorbers have a fibrous surrounding, with a gel-like core. If they shift or rupture, the affected disk will compress the spinal cord and interfere with the nerve impulses. The impact of a ruptured intervertebral disk and its severity depends on the part of the spinal cord that is affected. Neck pain is the most common symptom, because this part of the spinal column is most likely to be affected, although symptoms, such as incontinence, may emerge if the thoracolumbar region is injured.

A ruptured disk often occurs in dogs with short legs (see *Short Legs, Ruptured Disk,* right), but it can also affect a large dog. In this case, signs of a disk problem rarely emerge before middle age, and it is primarily the result of wear and tear. The symptoms are usually more progressive. The condition is often responsible for a slight dragging of the legs, but ultimately the legs can become paralyzed.

Diagnosis and Treatment

When an intervertebral disk is damaged, X-rays can reveal the severity of the problem. Your veterinarian can prescribe painkillers, as well as corticosteroids to ease the inflammation. It is important to keep your dog confined and prevent him from jumping so that the injury can heal, whether or not surgery is needed. The injury can reoccur in the future.

Short Legs, Ruptured Disk

Dachshunds, Pekingese, and other small, short-legged breeds are prone to a ruptured disk problem, and because dachshunds have an elongated body, they are especially at risk. The spinal column tends to flex, putting greater pressure on the disks. The situation is worse in an overweight dog. Once an intervertebral disk problem occurs, it can reoccur later in life.

Dachshunds and other high-risk breeds should always be exercised wearing a harness instead of a collar to avoid injury to their disks. It is also important to deter these dogs from jumping up onto chairs or climbing stairs, because these activities place the spinal column under more stress.

Strokes and Blood Clots

If the cerebrum at the front of the brain becomes damaged for any reason, there is a risk of hemorrhaging, which can lead to a stroke. Fortunately, strokes in dogs are rare, because they tend not to build up fatty tissue in their arteries in the way that humans do.

Symptoms similar to a stroke can result from a blood clot that forms elsewhere in the body. The clot can be carried in the bloodstream to the brain, where it leads to a blockage of a blood vessel. As a consequence, the brain cells in this area will not get enough oxygen and are likely to die, and the clot creates what is known as an infarction. The brain has a high requirement for oxygen, and a shortage of oxygen can have irreversible effects within 30 seconds.

Changes in the blood vessels, resulting in a loss of elasticity in their walls as the result of age, can also reduce the amount of oxygen being carried to areas of the brain. In severe cases this may cause the dog to collapse or show unexpected signs of paralysis, but in mild cases he may simply appear disoriented.

Preventing Further Strokes

The trigger for a stroke is often linked to another problem—for example, high blood pressure (hypertension) arising from chronic kidney failure (see pages 94–97). If an underlying cause for the stroke can be ascertained, then controlling the original problem will help to prevent a recurrence of a stroke in the future. Meanwhile, a brain scan should help to reveal the exact location and severity of the damage already caused.

Recovery

A dog is generally better at recovering from a stroke than a person because he is more reliant on his brain stem instead of the cerebrum. Although a dog is usually weak right after a stroke, his condition will often improve rapidly. In most cases the dog will not have any long-term paralysis.

Vestibular Disease

Disturbances of the vestibular system in the inner ear, which links the sensory input from the dog's environment with its coordination from the brain, produce symptoms that can be confused with strokes (see

Paws for thought...

After a stroke some dogs may develop a residual weakness that affects the limbs. However, most dogs will usually adjust to this problem with relative ease.

Symptoms of Vestibular Disease

- Nausea.

- Head tremors, with the dog's head being tilted to one side.

- Dog starts to move around in circles.

Symptoms of Vestibular Disease, opposite page). However, in this case, the cause may simply be the result of an ear infection, although it can also be indicative of hypothyroidism (see pages 130–31) or even a tumor. The symptoms will usually subside after several weeks, depending on their cause.

Seizures

When a dog has a seizure, which is also often referred to as a fit or convulsion, he may lose consciousness completely or partially, fall to the ground, and salivate profusely. His legs may also have a paddlelike movement. Seizures appear to be increasingly common in older dogs today, and a wide range of possible causes can be linked with other organs in the body, such as the kidneys and liver, as well as the endocrine system. Your veterinarian may perform a range of tests to identify the source of the problem and provide the most effective remedy. Further tests may be necessary to ensure there are no side effects arising from the treatment, particularly if epilepsy is diagnosed.

It may be possible to localize the problem, particularly if the dog's gait is affected. This suggests a problem in the cerebellum, the part of the brain concerned with movement. The cause may not always be clear, as in the case of a condition known as cerebellar abiotrophy that afflicts Brittany spaniel females between the age of 7 and 13. Unsteadiness on the feet and muscle tremors are often the first symptoms, with the dog walking with its head extended down in the direction of the ground. This progressive illness results in the dog losing its ability to walk.

Female Brittany spaniels may become unsteady on their feet and have muscle tremors, symptoms of cerebellar abiotrophy.

5 Steps to Handling a Seizure

1. Avoid being bitten accidentally.

2. Try to support your dog so he cannot hurt himself (but do not put anything in his mouth).

3. Be prepared for the fact that he may lose temporary control of his bladder and bowel functions.

4. Soothe your dog by speaking gently to him.

5. Seek veterinary advice without delay.

Degenerative illnesses of the brain

Dogs are living for much longer than in the past, so owners and veterinarians are now being faced by particular problems associated with a noticeable deterioration in the dog's mental state. Illnesses of this type are often referred to collectively as canine Alzheimer's disease. Although some of the changes seen in the brain are similar, this is not the same condition that can afflict elderly people. It is more accurately described as canine cognitive dysfunction (CCD).

There are a number of different indicators of CCD, which occurs as the result of a marked deterioration in the functioning capacity of the brain. Research has shown that these signs start at about 9 years old, with approximately two-thirds of dogs that are more than 14 years old being affected by them.

What Can Be Done?

Some of the changes seen in the brain of an elderly dog cannot be reversed, but there are treatments that can bring benefits in certain cases. A drug known as selegiline hydrochloride helps to reinforce the action of dopamine, a chemical occurring in the brain that is vital for the transmission of nerve impulses. Recent studies have shown that up to three-quarters of older dogs with symptoms of CCD may benefit from this medicine. Unfortunately, selegiline will only slow the rate of mental deterioration, but it can significantly increase the dog's quality of life by perhaps two years or more, with up to one-third of cases showing significant benefits from such therapy. This drug also seems to have a marked protective effect against cancer in older dogs (see pages 140–43).

Old-dog encephalitis

A condition known as old-dog encephalitis used to be a significant problem, but it has now become much less common because most dogs are routinely immunized against distemper. However, it can still occur in a dog that was not protected against this viral disease in puppyhood. A dog can contract distemper not just from other dogs, but also from various wild

Paws for thought...

Some pet food manufacturers have introduced special diets with antioxidants to help offset the effects of aging. Available on prescription, such foods can be beneficial if combined with plenty of mental stimulation, which can be achieved by playing with your dog and providing toys (see pages 58–59 and pages 64–65).

Symptoms of CCD

- Dog appears disoriented on occasions in the home environment.

- Lapses in housebreaking for which there is no obvious medical reason.

- Dog tends to be less responsive to people, especially in his immediate circle.

- Sleep patterns alter significantly, with the dog often barking repeatedly at night and becoming distressed.

- May display strange behavior patterns, such as walking in circles, or persistently nibbling at a particular area of his body.

animals, such as foxes and skunks. Although a young dog may be successfully nursed back to health in the initial illness, the disease may emerge later in life as old-dog encephalitis—and some dogs may not have shown previous signs. A warning indicator in a dog that had a distemper infection can be seen in the pads of his feet, which may be abnormally thick and badly cracked and furrowed. This is why distemper is also known as hard pad.

Not all dogs that have had distemper will develop old-dog encephalitis. In those that do, the cause of the problem is the presence of distemper virus within the dog's central nervous system. It causes inflammation of the dog's brain, which affects his movements. The symptoms (see *Symptoms of Old-Dog Encephalitis,* right) are worse if the dog becomes stressed for any reason. Anti-inflammatory drugs can help alleviate the symptoms, but there is no cure for this condition.

Symptoms of Old-Dog Encephalitis

- Loss of balance, which may cause your dog to fall over unexpectedly.

- A strange, high-stepping gait in old age.

An unresponsive dog is a sign of degenerative canine cognitive dysfunction. Disorientation is another indication of the condition.

The Eyes and Sight

Although the dog's sense of sight is important, dogs are less dependent than humans on this sense. Even if your pet's vision deteriorates significantly as he ages, he should be able to adjust well, particularly while he is in familiar surroundings.

Dogs can develop visual disturbances in two ways: if there is a problem that affects the structure of the eyes, or if the problem is in the nerve pathways that lead to the brain.

Cataracts

Degenerative changes occur in the eye because of aging, such as in the case of cataracts, a common problem. They develop when the lens starts to become cloudy. This may sometimes be linked with an illness elsewhere in the body, such as diabetes mellitus (see page 134–37), and one or both eyes can be affected. The only available treatment for cataracts is surgery, and this may not be suitable for all dogs. You will need to decide whether to have the lens removed and not replaced,

Light enters the eye through the pupil, with the iris changing in diameter so that when it is dark, it becomes wider, letting in more light. It can also narrow to prevent the dog from being blinded in bright light. The rays of light pass through the transparent lens and reach the retina at the back of the eye, which is where images form. These travel along the optic nerve to the brain, which forms a composite view of what the dog is seeing.

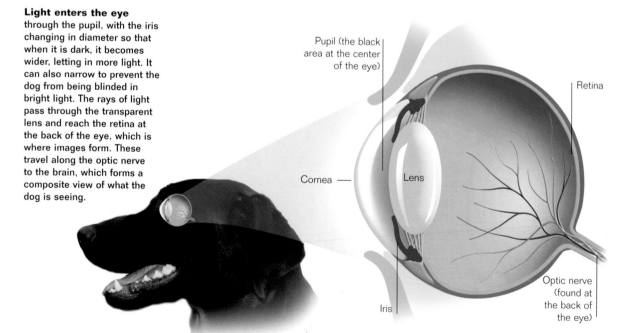

Pupil (the black area at the center of the eye)

Retina

Cornea

Lens

Iris

Optic nerve (found at the back of the eye)

which will make your dog long-sighted, reducing his close-up vision, or to have a new lens fitted to restore his sight as far as possible.

Glaucoma

A buildup in the pressure within the eye is responsible for glaucoma. There are no obvious symptoms, but your dog may become restless because he is in pain, and he will probably not be able to see clearly. Various medications can often help without recourse to surgery.

Treating Your Dog's Eyes

You may be nervous about treating your dog's eyes with drops or an ointment, but it is not difficult, particularly if you have someone who can hold your dog still for you. Start by tilting your dog's head upward, then steady his head and squeeze out the medication carefully. With drops there is a risk that your dog may blink at the wrong moment. If they did not reach the surface of the eye, try again.

In the case of an ointment, place the nozzle close to the eye to be treated, just as with the drops, and squeeze the tube gently to expel some of the medication so it falls onto the eye. It is important to prevent your dog from rubbing his face with his paws, because he can wipe away the medicine. Try to keep him still for a few moments until most of the ointment has dissolved into the eye.

Iris Atrophy

Sometimes the size of the pupils may vary from one eye to another because the colored area of the eye, known as the iris, is no longer able to adjust as it used to when the dog was younger. It may look disturbing, but it is not a significant handicap. Smaller breeds, particularly Chihuahuas, miniature schnauzers, and both toy and miniature poodles are most vulnerable.

No More Tears

Tear fluid is important in lubricating the surface of the eyes, but it can dry up in older dogs. This will have serious consequences, leaving an affected individual at risk of developing eye infections and damage to the cornea, which covers the surface of the eyes. A drug known as cyclosporine may help, but a more radical approach is surgery to connect one of the salivary glands to the eye, which will keep the surface of the cornea lubricated.

Cataracts give the lens in the eye an opaque, cloudy appearance. They can make it difficult for a dog to see.

Why Do Dogs Need Frequent Eye Treatments?

Ophthalmic medications usually need to be given perhaps three or four times a day, simply because they are being constantly washed out of the eye with tear fluid. This will drain away through a tiny opening hidden just inside the lower eyelid, near the nose, and passes into the nasal cavities.

The Ears and Hearing

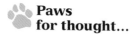
The appearance of a dog's ear provides some insight into his background. Breeds that hunt in undergrowth or swim have ears that hang down over the ear canal to protect the interior of their ears. Other breeds have erect ears, which can be more effective at trapping sound waves because of their upright shape.

A dog's ear can easily become infected. It is important to check your dog's ears throughout his life, because infections are often difficult to eliminate successfully and frequently reoccur. Chronic inflammation of this type can be linked to deafness. The most obvious sign of an ear infection will be your dog rubbing his ears more than usual.

Reduced hearing

As a dog grows older, his hearing inevitably declines, and ultimately he may go deaf. Tumors are the cause in some cases of deafness; in others, it may be environmental factors. A working gundog will often sustain damage to his hearing as a result of being constantly close to

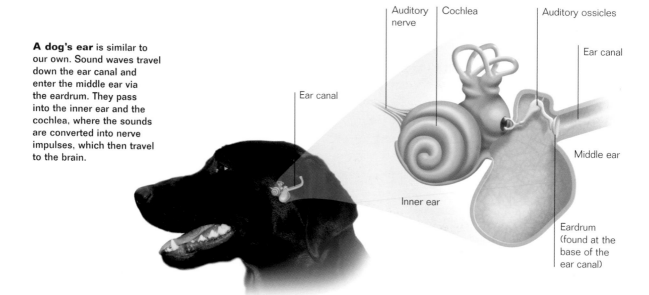

A dog's ear is similar to our own. Sound waves travel down the ear canal and enter the middle ear via the eardrum. They pass into the inner ear and the cochlea, where the sounds are converted into nerve impulses, which then travel to the brain.

Auditory nerve

Cochlea

Auditory ossicles

Ear canal

Ear canal

Middle ear

Inner ear

Eardrum (found at the base of the ear canal)

the noise of gunfire, while certain drugs, such as the antibiotic gentamicin, may occasionally trigger an adverse reaction that can result in deafness.

Dealing with Deafness

It is difficult for an owner to test if his dog has lost his hearing. Simply clapping close to his head will also generate air currents, and the dog may be responding to these instead of hearing any sound. However, your veterinarian can carry out a special test for deafness.

There is usually little that can be done to treat the problem, especially if the cause is simply old age. Fortunately, most dogs adapt well to losing their hearing. However, exercising your dog can become a problem, especially if he tends to run ahead, because it will be difficult to attract his attention. Roads also represent a greater danger. Nevertheless, you may be able to retrain your pet using hand signals (see pages 78–79), and a vibrating collar can also provide another way of communicating with a deaf dog. At night you may be able to teach your pet to come when he sees a flickering flashlight (see pages 84–85).

Hearing Aids

Canine hearing aids are available, but these need to fit deeper within the ear canal than those used by people because of the shape of the dog's ear canal. There is a risk that the hearing aid, by blocking off free airflow, can trigger an ear infection. It will take several weeks to train your dog to wear a hearing aid. You should then notice better behavioral responses from your dog as he becomes more alert and aware of his surroundings again. Nevertheless, although hearing aids for dogs exist, many simply will not wear them.

> ### Symptoms of Deafness
>
> - Less responsive than in the past.
> - Appears to be disobedient.
> - Tends to bark less and is quieter around the home.
> - Often sleeps for longer because he is not roused by noises.
> - Can be easily startled and may become more nervous.

Long, pendulous ears that trail down on some breeds, such as basset hounds and spaniels, are vulnerable to infections.

The Hormonal System

Hormones are chemical messengers, which are produced in one part of the body and carried by the blood to another area, where they produce their effect. There are various endocrine glands in the body, and these are responsible for producing different hormones to target different organs.

When there is a disruption to the hormonal system, such as the control mechanism breaking down, it can affect how much hormone a gland within the system produces. The resulting illness is described as "hyper" if there is too much hormone or, if the gland's output declines dramatically, the condition is referred to as "hypo."

The cause of the problem may not necessarily lie within the control mechanism in the brain. One of the glands may be damaged in some way, so it may not be functioning properly. The third possibility is that the target tissue itself may have become insensitive to the hormone, possibly because of treatment for another illness.

The dog's hormones are regulated by the hypothalamus in the brain. If the level needs to be increased, a signal is sent to the pituitary gland, which releases the trigger for glands elsewhere to make more hormones. Once the hormonal output has increased, the hypothalamus reduces its stimulation of the pituitary gland.

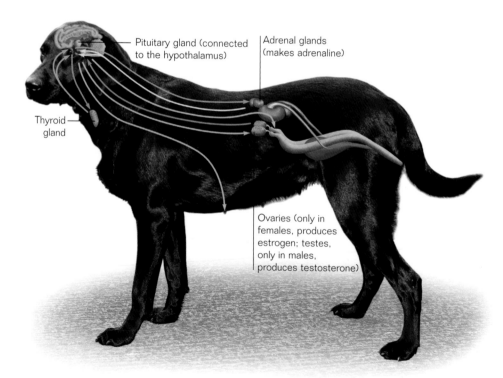

Pituitary gland (connected to the hypothalamus)

Adrenal glands (makes adrenaline)

Thyroid gland

Ovaries (only in females, produces estrogen; testes, only in males, produces testosterone)

When it comes to discovering the underlying cause, investigating problems involving the hormonal system can be difficult, and a number of conditions linked to the system are more likely to emerge in older dogs. However, it is often possible to provide effective long-term treatments—and even to reverse the signs of the illness.

The parathyroids

The parathyroid glands are located in the neck, lying close to the larger thyroid glands. They produce parathyroid hormone (PTH), which is critical in helping to ensure a healthy skeleton by regulating calcium stores in the body and stimulating its uptake from the digestive tract. If the level of PTH rises too high, the thyroid glands produce calcitonin, which should block further production of PTH.

A tumor can develop on the parathyroid glands and result in an excessive production of PTH—it can even override its control mechanism. As a consequence, the dog's skeleton will start to break down and the calcium level in the blood will start to rise accordingly. These tumors appear particularlly in dogs over eight years old, especially in keeshonden.

The signs at first may not be obvious, although sometimes there may be calcium stones in the urinary tract (see pages 92–93). An affected dog generally seems unwell—there is a loss of weight and lethargy, for example—and a blood test will probably reveal a low level of phosphorus in the circulation. If this condition, known as hyperparathyroidism, remains undetected, the bones will become weak, and those in the lower jaw will develop a rubbery texture. This loss of mineralization of the bone also causes the teeth to become loose, so eating will become painful for your dog.

Treatment of hyperparathyroidism may be possible. However, if a tumor is the cause, surgery can be hazardous. Instead, the tumor may be injected with alcohol to try to kill the malignant cells. The use of diuretics to flush the excess calcium out of the body, along with bicarbonate, which will bind with the calcium, are also particularly useful.

Keeshonden are at risk of developing a tumor on their parathyroid glands, leading to a breakdown of bones if left untreated.

Similar Symptoms, Other Causes

There can be a number of other causes underlying abnormally high levels of blood calcium, including cancer. Feeding your dog a poor diet can also replicate symptoms that are similar to hyperparathyroidism. If you provide your dog with nothing to eat other than prime steak, for example, which is a poor source of calcium—it is locked up in the body in the bones—then PTH output will increase significantly over time. The lack of dietary calcium will lead to the mineral being stripped from the dog's bones. This is known as secondary nutritional hyperparathyroidism. This is one reason why it is important to make sure you feed your dog a balanced diet (see pages 42–47).

Hypothyroidism

Thyroid function often declines from middle age onward, and underactive thyroids cause the disease known as hypothyroidism, which is the most common hormonal problem that affects dogs. It can be difficult to detect the early symptoms of this condition, partly because these can be confused with the aging process. Loss of vitality, weight gain, digestive problems, and neuromuscular disturbances can all be associated with a reduced hormonal output from the thyroid glands. However, there are also more obvious symptoms that may alert you to your dog's illness, such as unexplained hair loss, with the skin often starting to thicken and become more heavily pigmented.

A simple blood test should determine if your dog has hypothyroidism. If there is both a low thyroid hormone reading and an elevated level of thyroid-stimulating hormone, which triggers the thyroid glands to produce their hormones, this suggests the glands are not functioning normally and their production is suppressed.

Treating Hypothyroidism

It is a straightforward process to treat hypothyroidism. Your veterinarian will prescribe medication in pill form to make up for the deficiency. You should find that the signs of your dog's illness will start to disappear, but it may take several weeks for a noticeable improvement. Your dog will need to be treated every day for the rest of his life, but the pills are not expensive. Further blood tests may be required to monitor your dog's progress.

Breeds Susceptible to Hypothyroidism

- Old English sheepdog

- Irish setter

- Miniature schnauzer

- Great Dane

- Golden retriever (below)

Boxers are one of the breeds susceptible to Cushing's disease, which can be detected by a symmetrical pattern of hair loss.

Virtually all cases of hypothyroidism are due to degenerative changes in the dog's thyroid glands, but on rare occasions a pituitary tumor may be the underlying cause of the problem. This usually affects the functioning of other endocrine glands, too, not only the thyroids.

Cushing's disease

Hypothyroidism is not the only hormonal cause of hair loss and skin changes seen in older dogs. These symptoms can also occur if a dog has Cushing's disease, which affects the adrenal glands, located near the kidneys. This disease usually affects dogs between 7 and 12 years old. The Labrador retriever, Boston terrier, beagle, German shepherd, and boxer are the breeds most susceptible to this condition.

Part of the adrenal glands produces cortisol, which is a natural corticosteroid. If the pituitary gland starts to produce an excessive amount of adrenocorticotrophic hormone (ACTH), this in turn causes overproduction of corticosteroids in the adrenal glands. Symmetrical hair loss on both sides of the body, a heightened susceptibility to skin infections, and an increasingly potbellied appearance are common signs associated with Cushing's disease. In such cases it is important to determine whether the cause lies in the pituitary gland or the adrenals so that the correct treatment can be given.

Natural Remedies

Seaweed powder, sometimes sold as kelp, is a rich natural source of iodine, which is an essential component of thyroid hormones. It can be sprinkled over wet food as a supplement and helps to guard against goiter. This is an enlargement of the thyroids resulting from a dietary deficiency of iodine.

Breeds Susceptible to Addison's Disease

- Leonberger
- Standard poodle (below)
- Portuguese water spaniel
- Nova Scotia duck tolling retriever

Addison's disease

Also known as hypoadrenocorticism, Addison's disease occurs when the production of corticosteroids is markedly reduced. It tends to be most common in female dogs, with symptoms emerging in middle age, and it is more prevalent in some breeds than others, suggesting that it might be an inherited condition. Addison's disease is thought to be an autoimmune disease, caused by the dog's body reacting to block the output of corticosteroids.

The symptoms of Addison's disease can be vague, consisting of loss of appetite, vomiting, and lethargy. If the dog is put under too much stress—for example, by doing a long walk on a hot day with no water to drink—the lack of corticosteroids can be fatal, causing an irregular heartbeat, shaking, and shivering, and the dog can collapse. However, if the condition is diagnosed, regular treatment with corticosteroid drugs should ensure that an affected dog remains in good health.

The reproductive system

A female dog that has not been spayed is likely to have regular periods of heat, with males retaining a corresponding interest in mating, until the end of her life. Although the likelihood of conception falls dramatically in an older dog, it is still possible. If your female dog has not been spayed, you should consider it, not only to prevent unwanted puppies but also to prevent a pregnancy late in life, which can have detrimental effects on the dog's health. Spaying your dog can also keep her from developing certain hormonal problems. The first is an increasing risk of a false pregnancy (see page 65). Although it can be alarming, it is not life-threatening, unlike the condition known as pyometra.

Symptoms of Pyometra

(Occurs only in unspayed females.)

- Drinks more than usual.
- Loss of appetite.
- Vomiting.
- Discharge from the vagina, which may be bloody.

Pyometra

An age-related illness, pyometra usually occurs in a female dog over five years old. The signs of pyometra follow the estrous period—when the dog is in heat—typically about a month to six weeks later. The telltale symptom is often a discharge from the dog's vagina, which may be bloody and can contain pus as a result of an infection that has developed higher up the reproductive tract in the uterus. This is known as an "open pyometra." If the cervix at the mouth of the womb is closed, the uterus will swell up with this toxic material, which becomes trapped. This may cause the abdomen to appear swollen.

The Cause of Pyometra

This disorder is caused in part by hormones in the dog's body. Progesterone produced in the ovaries after ovulation acts on the uterine tissue, causing the outer layer, known as the endometrium, to develop. This ensures that it will be able to nourish the fertilized eggs before the embryos create a placental attachment in the mother's body. In the case of a pyometra, instead of the production of progesterone stopping as normal, it continues. If mating has not occurred and bacteria invade the uterus, passing up from the vagina, it can trigger an infection.

> ### Reducing the Risk of Pyometra
>
> If your female dog is not spayed, it is not recommended to:
>
> - Treat your dog with progesterone compounds to delay a period of heat because you are going away and want to avoid her from coming into heat at the kennels.
>
> - Give your dog an estrogen compound to prevent a pregnancy if she has mated during a period of heat. Although it does not impact directly on the uterus, it makes the tissue more reactive to the effects of progesterone.

If you suspect that your dog has a pyometra, seek immediate veterinary advice. Although pyometra can sometimes be treated with fluid therapy and antibiotics, the dog is likely to have another attack during a subsequent period of heat. Therefore, the most effective treatment is spaying.

Case History

A Solution for Susie

Susie, an eight-year-old crossbreed, was spayed during her last heat because she had pyometra. However, the dog continued to experience the symptoms just after the time when her next heat would be due. She had what is described as "stump pyometra," where an infection developed in the small portion of the uterus that was left in the abdomen during the surgery, which is a normal procedure. Her veterinarian was able to treat Susie by giving her a course of antibiotics and fluids. However, if this hadn't worked successfully, then further surgery would had been required to overcome the problem.

Diabetes mellitus

This hormonal illness is caused by an abnormality in the body's ability to deal with sugar present in the blood, which is used by the cells as a source of energy. In normal circumstances the islets of Langerhans, which are located in the pancreas—a gland near the small intestine—release the hormone known as insulin into the bloodstream. This stimulates the uptake of sugar by the cells, preventing a concentration of sugar from building up in the bloodstream. As the blood glucose falls, another hormone, known as glucagon, is released in place of insulin to encourage the blood sugar level to rise again.

In cases of diabetes it may be that the pancreas is no longer able to function effectively, so the output of insulin into the circulation declines. This is described as Type 1 diabetes. Alternatively, if the cells throughout the body lose their ability to respond to insulin, then Type 2 diabetes will result. Irrespective of the cause, the symptoms are the same. There is an accumulation of sugar in the bloodstream, and it reaches a level where it starts to be lost in the dog's urine, which then develops a distinctive sweet odor. The high concentration of sugar in the blood will cause a dog to start drinking much more than usual, and his urinary output rises accordingly, too.

Symptoms of Diabetes

- Increased thirst and urinary output.

- Bad breath.

- Lethargy.

- Loss of weight.

- Cataracts in both eyes.

- Vulnerability to infections, especially cystitis—an inflammation of the bladder—because of the presence of glucose in the urine.

Frequent urination was a problem for Angus, a seven-year-old West Highland white terrier, before being diagnosed with diabetes.

The cells react by breaking down the body's fat stores, because they can no longer access glucose, and this produces what are known as ketone bodies. These cause the dog's breath to develop an odor similar to nail polish remover, as the level of acetone in the blood rises. Before long, if your dog is not treated with insulin, he will lapse into a coma and may die.

Diagnosing Diabetes

A simple urine test, performed by using a dipstick in a urine sample, will indicate the presence of sugar. A blood test will also confirm the diagnosis. It will indicate a raised sugar level, but more significantly, it will show whether the blood insulin level is low, indicating Type 1, or high, which confirms that your dog has Type 2 diabetes.

Your veterinarian may ask you to take a urine sample from your dog. If you use a jar as a container, make sure it did not contain a sugary item, such as jam, and wash it out thoroughly; any trace left behind will affect the result. You can catch the urine by placing a clean plastic tray near the dog at the appropriate moment, then pour the urine straight into the container. Only a small amount of urine is needed, about a few tablespoons.

Overweight Dogs and Diabetes

Diabetes is on the rise in dogs, particularly Type 2, which is linked with obesity. This is one reason why it is important to ensure that your pet does not become overweight as he grows older. It is thought that the fat cells in the body are affected by the stress hormone cortisol, and this blocks their ability to respond to insulin. In fact, there is a third type of diabetes, which can be induced by excessive use of corticosteroid drugs—these are similar hormones—for treatment of inflammation and similar conditions.

Diabetes insipidus

When the term "diabetes" is used, it often refers to diabetes mellitus, or sugar diabetes. However, there is a rare form completely unrelated to the pancreas or insulin. It is known as diabetes insipidus and results from the failure of the hypothalamus in the brain to produce antidiuretic hormone (ADH), or the kidneys fail to respond to ADH, which causes the dog to produce more urine than normal. Treatment involves giving an ADH substitute as eyedrops or nose drops.

Breeds Susceptible to Diabetes

Small breeds are most vulnerable to diabetes, particularly the following, with the incidence of diabetes being much higher in unspayed females:

- Cairn terriers
- Beagles
- Dachshunds (below)
- Schnauzers
- Miniature poodles

Treating diabetes mellitus

There are a number of steps that need to be taken to control diabetes. Although treatment revolves around giving your dog insulin, it is also important to slim your dog down if he is overweight, especially in the case of Type 2 diabetes. This alone can make a significant difference, especially if combined with dietary changes, too.

A Diet for Diabetics

The carbohydrate part of your dog's food intake is important because different carbohydrates are digested at different rates. For example, if you simply rely on rice as a source of carbohydrate for your pet, it will be broken down into glucose, which is absorbed into the body relatively quickly after the meal, causing a spike in insulin production. However, barley is digested much more slowly than rice. By making sure your dog's food contains a range of carbohydrates, they will be broken down and absorbed at different rates. This ensures that the body's insulin response is correspondingly lower and extends over a longer period of time.

Your veterinarian may recommend one of the specially formulated prescription foods available for dogs that have diabetes. These provide a regulated dietary means of helping to control this illness.

A Family Commitment

When you have children and a diabetic dog, you need to explain to them that they must not offer him treats of any kind, especially sweet ones. It is also important that they tell you if your dog has stolen any food left around the home, such as chocolate, because it can have a serious effect on his health, particularly because chocolate can be toxic to all dogs—not just diabetic ones.

Insulin

There are various types of insulin available, and it may take some experimentation on the part of your veterinarian to find the most suitable type and dose for your dog. You need to develop a precise routine, too, by feeding your dog twice a day at specific times. These will be preceded by an injection of insulin, and giving a standard

Paws for thought...

Store insulin in a refrigerator. When preparing to give your dog an injection, do not shake the insulin because this creates foam and affects its level of activity. Instead, tip the container up gently so that its contents are mixed, then draw off the necessary volume slowly into the syringe; measure it carefully.

Too Much Insulin

If you give your dog too much insulin, he will become hypoglycemic, which can cause him to collapse as his blood sugar falls to a critically low level. This condition can also be triggered if your dog becomes overexcited. For this type of emergency, always keep a jar of honey available. You can give the honey to your dog by mouth, or you can mix the honey with a little water and give it orally in a syringe. The sugar in honey is absorbed quickly into the bloodstream, which helps to raise the glucose level.

dose will be essential. Once stabilized, diabetic dogs can enjoy a good quality of life as long as you follow the treatment recommended by your veterinarian. However, if your dog has cataracts (see pages 124–25), these will not be reversible, even with insulin treatment.

Administering insulin is easier than most dog owners expect. The needle used is fine, making the procedure painless. Your veterinarian will show you how to inject the insulin into the scruff of your dog's neck. Initially, it will help if someone else holds your dog while you concentrate on giving the injection. Using a new needle every time ensures that it will go through the skin easily, and be sure that it is attached firmly to the syringe before giving the injection. If you want to practice your technique, the best way is to use an orange—but use water instead of insulin.

Caution

If you have a diabetic dog, do not use semi-moist foods of any type. These contain a relatively high level of sugar, which serves as a preservative but is not recommended for a diabetic.

Borzois are so tall that their heads are at table height, so it is easy for seven-year-old Teddy to grab a snack. Make sure you and your family keep all food out of your dog's reach at all times.

Cancer

As a dog grows older, the risk that he will develop cancer increases significantly. It has been estimated that cancer accounts for half the deaths of all dogs over 10 years old. Nevertheless, there have been significant advances in the treatment of cancer in dogs recently, and early diagnosis and treatment can dramatically increase the likelihood of your dog living a full life.

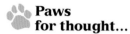
**Paws
for thought...**

Certain cancers, notably those affecting the lungs and tonsils, are more common in dogs living in urban areas. These cancers are thought to be linked with air pollution.

Cancer is a general term covering a wide range of illnesses, and any organ system in the body is potentially at risk. Some breeds are also far more susceptible to cancers than others, and the boxer is by far the most vulnerable. There are also specific tumors most likely to be encountered in particular breeds of dog. Large breeds, such as the Irish wolfhound, are especially vulnerable to bone tumors known as osteosarcomas. The sex of the dog and whether it has been neutered are also factors influencing the dog's susceptibility to different forms of cancer. Females are at greater risk of developing benign fatty tumors called lipomas, compared with their male counterparts, and they are far more vulnerable to tumors of the mammary glands, too.

Malignant or Benign?

In all cases, cancer is the result of the uncontrolled and often rapid growth of groups of abnormal cells in the body. These are unrecognized by the body's own defense mechanisms, which allows them to continue developing unchecked. The growths can be divided into two categories.

Benign cancers grow slowly and do not invade the surrounding tissue. They are usually less threatening to your dog's health, although they can grow large and compress neighboring tissues, which can result in discomfort. Benign skin tumors are also at risk of being injured during grooming, which will cause them to bleed, so they should not be ignored. The only way to be certain that a tumor is in fact benign is by doing a microscopic examination of tissue samples.

Symptoms of Cancer

These depend to some extent on the organ system that is affected, but malignant cancers in particular may also produce a number of generally nonspecific symptoms. Typical indicators may include:

- Unexplained weight loss.

- Increased thirst.

- Recurrent fever.

- Swellings on or in the body.

Malignant growths are serious because they are more invasive. They can spread, or "metastasize," to other parts of the body, often through the bloodstream, creating secondary tumors. About every 4 out of 10 cancers in dogs are malignant.

Protecting Your Dog

It is not possible to prevent all cancers, but there are some that can be avoided more easily than others. Avoid smoky places—cigarette smoke can cause cancer in dogs. Do not allow your dog to sit outside in the sun for long periods in the middle of the day, when the sun will be at its hottest. Otherwise, your dog will have an increased risk of developing the skin tumor known as malignant melanoma. Pale-coated breeds are especially susceptible, because of the lack of protective dark melanin pigment in their skin. A particularly common site for a tumor to develop is on the ear, because ears often have a relatively sparse covering of hair, leaving the skin more exposed to the sun's harmful ultraviolet rays. Try protecting them with a canine sunblock, which is available at pet stores and via the Internet.

Causes of Tumors

The underlying reasons for cancer are not clearly understood in all cases, but there are a number of factors that may be implicated. These include:

- A genetic predisposition to developing certain types of tumor.

- Some viral infections.

- Environmental factors, including sunlight and air pollution.

- Hormonal factors.

Spaying a female at an early age will protect her from developing mammary tumors. Spaying before her first period of heat will halve the risk of your dog developing this particular type of tumor, but neutering later in life can also be beneficial. Females that are not spayed have a sevenfold increase of developing mammary tumors compared with those that have undergone this surgery.

A dog with white fur, such as nine-year-old Wrangle, a retired sled dog, is more susceptible to developing skin cancer.

Common types of cancer

There are many different types of cancer, some of which are rare. The specific symptoms will relate to the area of the body where the cancer is present. In the throat region the dog may have difficulty swallowing; however, in the case of a bone tumor, known as an osteosarcoma, that affects the hind leg, lameness will be common. This is why it is important to be vigilant about your pet's health and seek advice without delay if you notice any unusual symptoms.

Skin Tumors

One of the most conspicuous types of cancer, skin tumors develop on the surface of the body. Especially in the early stages, they can be obscured by fur and may only be detected when you are stroking your dog or grooming him. Size is not an indication of malignancy, so all bumps should be seen by a veterinarian. Older dogs often develop lipomas, which can be quite large lumps of benign fatty tissue that form under the skin. These can be removed quite easily by surgery.

Mammary Tumors

These tumors are common in unspayed females from middle age onward. They show up as abnormal lumps near the teats, but they do not cause pain. However, there is also an aggressive form of breast cancer that affects the rear teats, which spreads rapidly into the groin area and causes considerable discomfort. Surgery is required to remove these tumors, and although more than 50 percent are benign, there is a risk of malignant tumors metastasizing into the nearby

Paws for thought...

Not every lump on the body is necessarily a form of cancer. If a hair follicle becomes blocked, it prevents sebum, which acts as a skin moisturizer, from passing out of the associated gland to the surface of the skin. This swelling is known as a sebaceous cyst. These are common, particularly in cocker spaniels.

Unspayed females are more susceptible to tumors developing near the teats.

lymph nodes, which is why these may be removed in cases where the tumor is suspected to be malignant. Mammary tumors can also spread to the lungs and cause secondary bone tumors. Male dogs may develop mammary tumors, too, but these are rare cases.

Lymphosarcoma

A swelling just under the skin can also be an early indication of a cancer of the lymphatic system, known as lymphosarcoma or lymphoma. This is actually the most common blood cancer in dogs, but it often responds well to surgery, where the diseased lymph node is removed. A course of chemotherapy may follow with the goal of achieving remission so the cancer does not return, although this type of cancer may be permanent. A high-fat diet may also be beneficial when treating this type of tumor (see pages 142–43).

Taking your dog to the vet

If you suspect there is something wrong, your veterinarian will need to examine the dog and ask you questions about his symptoms. He may palpate, or feel, body organs to try to locate a tumor, although ultrasound and X-ray examinations will be helpful in determining a tumor's overall size and location. After his examination, the veterinarian may simply recommend surgery to remove the tumor; however, in other cases he may want to take a biopsy—where a sample of the tissues is removed so it can be examined under a microscope by a specialist—before determining the most appropriate type of treatment (see pages 142–43).

Routine Monitoring

Regular checkups and blood tests can help to detect the presence of cancers. For example, if your dog has lymphosarcoma, there can be damage to the bone. This will mean that there will be a raised level of calcium in your dog's blood, which will show up in a routine blood test. However, this can be a feature of other conditions, such as hyperthyroidism (see pages 128–30), and also another type of tumor that tends to be more prevalent in elderly dogs, which affects the anal sacs that lie just within the rectum. It then becomes a matter for your veterinarian to identify the underlying cause of the raised calcium by doing other tests. Because of these other possiblities, your veterinarian may need to perform several tests before he can reach a diagnosis.

Dealing with Cancer

There are often difficult decisions to make in terms of an old dog and cancer therapy. In a case involving osteosarcoma, you may be faced with the decision to have your dog's leg amputated or to have him put to sleep. Dogs can survive and adapt remarkably well to life on three legs, especially if they are not overweight. However, if you are worried about how an amputation will affect your dog, ask your veterinarian if you can speak with owners whose dogs have had this surgery to help you understand how your dog might adapt.

Natural Remedies

The demands of the cancer cells for nutrients from the body to support their growth mean that dogs will lose weight. Increasing the amount of fat in your dog's food, so it forms up to 50 percent of the diet, may help to combat the cancer, because this food source, unlike glucose, does not provide the cancerous cells with an energy source. Zinc supplements may also be helpful, but first discuss dietary changes with your veterinarian.

Cancer treatment

An increasing number of treatments can be used to combat cancer in dogs, depending partly on the type of cancer, its severity, and where it is located in the body, as well as the overall state of your dog's health. Sometimes more than one method may be used in combination for this purpose.

Surgery

In many cases surgery remains the first option for treating cancer, particularly when the tumor is thought to be benign. This means that it is possible to remove the entire growth easily. However, surgery is a more difficult procedure when removing a malignant tumor because the cancer often invades the surrounding tissues. This is partly why early recognition increases the likelihood of a successful outcome—the tumor can be cut out more easily with some of the surrounding healthy tissue so there will be less risk of recurrence.

Surgery on a malignant tumor carries the risk that cutting into it may result in tiny fragments being carried off in the bloodstream, which will lead to tumors forming elsewhere in the body. There are also parts of the body where it is more difficult to perform surgery, such as the perineal region below the tail, which has a high blood supply.

Chemotherapy

Chemicals, such as cell-killing, or cytotoxic, drugs, are also used to treat cancer in dogs. This method can be particularly useful in cases where the cancer is diffuse, or has spread widely, as in the case of leukemia, a cancer of the white blood cells. However, because of the toxic nature of these drugs, chemotherapy can have adverse side effects. It is important that there is ongoing monitoring both before and during treatment, and particularly in old dogs, it is not always possible to use this type of treatment. For example, the anticancer drug cyclophosphamide is not safe in dogs that have evidence of liver failure or already have anemia, because it depresses the production of blood cells, and it can have harmful effects on the kidneys, too. Dogs generally do not lose their fur when undergoing chemotherapy.

Immunotherapy

Corticosteroids, such as prednisolone, have been used to treat some cancers, such as those of the lymphatic system, but they can have

Irish wolfhounds are one of the breeds that are susceptible to bone cancer. Early treatment can lead to a favorable outcome.

undesirable side effects on the pancreas and the body's adrenal glands. Research is currently under way to try to improve the body's natural immune mechanisms to fight cancer more effectively.

Radiotherapy

Where surgery of any type would be impractical, radiotherapy may be the only option. It is often used in cases of bone cancer, but because of the specialized equipment used and the associated safety precautions, you will probably be referred to a veterinary school by your veterinarian for this treatment, which relies on heavy doses of X-rays to kill the tumor.

Choosing a Treatment

It is important to match the treatment carefully to the type of cancer, because not all cancers respond equally well to the same method of treatment. For example, cryosurgery is not suitable for treating cancerous warts because they contain little fluid and cannot be killed easily by freezing. Chemotherapy is not suitable for treating osteosarcoma, or bone cancer.

Cryosurgery

A different type of surgery, known as cryosurgery, has been developed that entails the use of a probe applied to the diseased tissue, which freezes the cells with liquid nitrogen. Cryosurgery is especially useful for superficial tumors, including some of those that occur in the mouth. Several treatment sessions can be given in succession, but it takes time for the diseased tissue to slough off, or shed away, after being frozen in this way and for healing to occur.

Surgery Aftercare

When you pick up your dog after surgery, the veterinarian will give you instructions for his postoperative care, along with any medication that he may need. Follow the instructions carefully to ensure that your pet recovers without any complications—and do not hesitate to ask any questions if you are unsure about anything.

Dogs often recover surprisingly quickly from surgery. However, in some cases, especially after major surgery, you may have to wait for perhaps a day or two following the operation before your dog can return home. This is not an indication that there was a problem with the surgery; your veterinarian needs to monitor his condition closely so that if any deterioration occurs, he can take immediate action to safeguard his welfare.

What to Expect

When your dog does come home, he is likely to be able to walk and will be over the worst effects of the anesthetic. He may be hungry and might also want a drink. However, the stress of the surgery and being away from home may also mean that he will want to sleep after a cursory roam around on familiar territory.

Assuming that the home is warm, there will probably be no need to provide extra warmth. If the house is a little cold, there are gentle pet heaters that you can obtain to put at the base of your dog's basket, complete with metal casing to protect the power cord. These are safer than a hot water bottle, which can burn his skin—and your dog might puncture the bottle with his teeth, soaking his basket with hot water.

If your dog has stitches as a result of his operation, you may need to keep him from jumping up while the wound heals. Your dog may try to chew his dressing, and if he pulls it off, he will probably lick the wound beneath. It has been suggested that allowing your dog to behave in this way can aid healing, but it can also lead to the stitches being pulled out and the wound being opened. Some dogs appear more determined to behave in this way than others. If your pet will

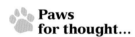
Paws for thought...

If you have another dog, try to keep your pets apart at first, because any energetic play—which is normal after dogs have been separated for some time—can easily open up the wound and lengthen his recovery.

not desist from trying to reach the wound, you may need to acquire a surgical, or so-called Elizabethan, collar for him.

Medication

Depending on the type of surgery, the veterinarian may prescribe medication. Pills or liquid medicines must be given regularly at the stated times. (For instructions on how to give your dog medication, see pages 19 and 27.) If you forget to give your dog a dose, do not give him a double dose because this could be harmful—instead, check with your veterinarian for advice. Be sure to read the storage instructions for the medicine, too. Pills usually simply need to be kept dry, out of reach of any children, and away from sunlight, but some liquid medicines need to be stored in a refrigerator.

Monitoring Your Dog

Even elderly dogs will generally recuperate without major problems from surgery, but keep a watch on your dog.

- Is he eating and drinking properly?

- Is he urinating as normal?

- Is he alert?

- Are his dressings in place?

You should contact your veterinarian without delay if any discharge is noticeable around the dressing or any unpleasant smell develops around it. You can also contact him if you have any other concerns.

After surgery your dog will probably need plenty of rest. Don't expect him to participate in any demanding activities.

CHAPTER 7 Journey's End

Life can be uncertain, so try to enjoy your dog's company every day, especially if he has a chronic illness. In spite of your best efforts—and those of your veterinarian—there will come a time when your dog's condition weakens and there will be little else that can be done for him. This places a difficult responsibility on you, but you will probably know deep down when the time has come to say good-bye to your pet.

You may be spared having to make this painful decision if your pet passes away quietly at home. However, this itself can bring its own trauma because there is no opportunity to say a proper farewell, and the shock can enhance the accompanying sense of loss. The important thing to remember at this difficult time is that you are not alone; in fact, there are some things you can do to help overcome your feelings of loss.

Making the Decision to
Say Good-bye

Your dog's well-being will be the most important factor in deciding when the time has come to say good-bye.

It is never easy to decide when your dog's condition has deteriorated to the point where he is suffering. Sometimes it can be helpful to discuss the circumstances with other family members, as well as with your veterinarian, especially if you are unsure.

Your veterinarian will not be able to make the decision to put your dog to sleep; that decision is yours alone. But at least you can receive professional advice from someone who is familiar with your dog's health. You also need to consider your dog's overall comfort and quality of life. *Is the Time Right?* (see below) provides some questions to ask yourself. If the answers to these questions are mostly positive, your pet's underlying illness or his advancing years is probably not seriously compromising his quality of life. But if the answers are mostly negative, your dog might be suffering some discomfort.

When the Time Comes

Once you have decided that it will be best for your dog to be put to sleep, you should make the necessary arrangements with your veterinarian. This will entail signing a consent form. Once you have brought your dog to the veterinarian, there is no need to stay if you feel this would be too distressing, both for you and your pet. Simply say good-bye and leave him with the veterinarian. Although you may feel that you have abandoned your pet, this is often the better option, simply because your dog will instinctively sense your distress and may thus become more upset.

A Painless Drug

When the veterinarian puts the dog to sleep by injecting a drug, it will be painless—this is known as euthanasia. The drug simply has the

---

Is the Time Right?

There are a number of questions that you may want to reflect upon when reaching a decision that involves euthanasia. Ask yourself:

- Can your dog still move around without great difficulty?

- Does he get up to see you when you come in?

- Does he ask to go outside to relieve himself?

- Is he still eating well?

- Does he take an obvious interest in what is going on around him?

effect of an overdose of anesthetic. To give the injection, a small area of fur will be clipped off the front or hind leg. The drug will be injected into the bloodstream through a vein, and the dog will fall asleep almost instantly. If you are present, you can help to hold your dog while the veterinarian gives the injection and then checks that it has taken effect and the heart has stopped beating.

After the injection has been given, there may be a few involuntary muscle spasms that cause your dog to twitch, but this is not an indication that he is still alive. There is often also a loss of bowel or bladder control.

> ## The Last Day
>
> The last hours of your dog's life can be enjoyable ones for him. Forget about work commitments and give your dog plenty of attention. Try to make him as comfortable as possible. Let him sleep in your bed if you've not allowed him to do so before. And indulge him with his favorite food—even if it had been forbidden before to keep his weight under control. Make sure all the family members—and other pets—have some time together.

Passing Away at Home

It may be that you need to call your veterinarian to put your dog to sleep at home, particularly if he is large or difficult to move. Bear in mind that you might find this process more distressing in your home because you may link the room with your pet's passing. The loss of bladder and bowel control is also more easily handled at your veterinarian's office than at home.

A Natural Death

Sometimes a dog dies naturally at home, perhaps collapsing or in his sleep. This can be a complete surprise to his owner because there are not always signs of a health problem. If you find your dog is immobile and looking as though he is asleep but his chest isn't moving and you can't find a heartbeat, your pet has passed away. As with euthanasia, the contents of your dog's bladder and bowel will probably have been voided, so you may need to clean around your dog. You can place him on a clean towel, blanket, or sheet. Call your veterinarian to discuss what to do with the body (see pages 150–51).

In the last days, abandon the rules and pamper your dog. Let your dog know how much you love him.

The First Days After
Your Loss

It should not be surprising to find that losing your dog has left a significant gap in your life. After all, your pet has been a central part of your life for many years, being a constant companion through both good times and bad. Grieving for the loss of your pet is normal, even if friends who have not experienced the companionship of a dog may find this strange.

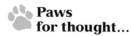

Paws for thought...

It may be better to dispose of your dog's bed, toys, and other items as soon as you can, because they can bring painful memories. However, you may want to put aside a keepsake, such as a favorite toy.

Each person faced with the death of their dog will have a different approach to coming to terms with the grief. Some days will be better than others and there is no established timescale. The situation is often worse if your pet dies suddenly, simply because of the shock. Having your dog put to sleep at least allows you time to say goodbye. Initially, you'll also have practical matters to consider, such as what to do with your dog's body and his belongings.

The Grieving Process

Be prepared for the fact that there are several stages that often form part of the grieving process.

- First, there is the overwhelming sense of loss.

- You may then go through a stage of feeling angry, perhaps blaming your veterinarian—however irrational this may be in hindsight—believing that more could have been done for your dog. You may blame yourself, too, and become irritable, even short-tempered, with family and friends.

- Gradually, there will be the realization that there is nothing that can be done to bring your pet back. Ultimately, the loss of your dog will start to recede from the forefront of your mind, although he will still feature in your thoughts.

- Ultimately, you will be left with fond memories of what you shared together, combined with a sense of sadness.

Making Arrangements

The first decision you need to make is what to do with your pet's remains. If you want, your veterinarian will be able to organize a cremation, or you can choose to handle the arrangements yourself. You might want to book a space for your dog in a pet cemetery, where you can visit him.

Alternatively, you can arrange an individual cremation and have his ashes interred with a headstone. The final decision is a matter of personal choice, but if you want to assume responsibility for your pet's remains, you will need to investigate the options that are available in your area.

Your Family

If you have children, you will also need to explain what has happened to the family dog, and obviously, this discussion will be influenced by their age. It can be a difficult issue for young children to understand, and at first they may continue to ask when your dog is coming back. Try to explain what has happened and answer their questions as much as you can. It may be upsetting at times, but do not feel that you have to hold back your feelings entirely in front of them. It may be that this is their first direct experience of death, and they will need to learn how to grieve.

Bereavement Counselor

If you find that you are being overwhelmed by grief and you don't have a partner or friend to turn to, professional pet bereavement counselors are available. Your veterinarian can provide you with the name of one in your area. Do not hesitate to ask for contact details at an early stage because, strange as it may sound, knowing that help is available can actually give you strength. Try to keep busy to help you get through the day.

> ### The Surviving Companion
>
> If you have another, younger dog, he may be disoriented by the loss of his companion. Try to reassure him by keeping to your normal routine of taking him out for walks and similar activities. He may be less interested in playing for a time, but try to prevent him from sitting around for long periods.

Your dog's companion will need special attention to help him adjust to the loss of his friend.

A dog's departure is often the first time a child experiences bereavement.

Moving
Forward

There are a number of options you may want to consider that may help you overcome your sense of loss. It is important to try to do something positive rather than just feeling depressed. This might mean making some type of memorial for your dog or caring for a new one.

Consider putting together a photo album as a way to look back over your dog's life. If you have an artistic side, you can make a painting of your pet or writing a poem or essay about him. The Internet may provide comfort and inspiration as well (see *Memorial Website,* opposite page).

Memorial Website

If you have a computer and access to the Internet, you may want to create a Web page in your dog's memory. Even if you do not have the expertise to set up an electronic page yourself, there are "In Memoriam" sites for pets on the Internet that allow you to post a photograph and include some words about your dog.

The Internet may also bring you comfort by providing an opportunity to see that you are not alone in facing this type of grief—many people have undergone a similar experience. This may be comforting if you are having difficulty dealing with your loss.

Starting Again

You will probably go through a stage of thinking there will never be another dog like your previous pet and that you cannot replace him—this is quite true. However, there will hopefully come a time when you feel that you may want to enjoy the companionship of another dog. Only you will know when you have reached this stage. Some people feel the house is empty without a dog and acquire a new pet soon afterward; however, others prefer to wait for perhaps several months or even longer. Obtaining another dog should help you to overcome your feelings of grief more easily, simply because your new pet will be demanding your time and attention, distracting you from your thoughts.

Too Old to Start Again?

Older people sometimes feel it would be unfair to acquire another dog because of their age. However, if you fit into this category, there's no need to let your age be a barrier that deprives you of the

enjoyment of canine companionship. Indeed, it can open up a new aspect of dog ownership: helping the homeless dog population. Rescue organizations are continuously working to find homes for them, but their funds are limited and keeping a dog in a kennel is an expensive option.

Many organizations try to maintain a network of caregivers who want to care for a dog until he can be found a permanent home. If you are able to take in a dog on a short-term basis, you will be helping to keep him out of a kennel, giving him affection, and hopefully guiding him toward a secure future. Alternatively, you can volunteer to become a dog walker for a rescue organization or for an owner who is ill—look for organizations within your area. You could also look into adopting an older dog (see pages 20–21).

Choosing a New Dog

If you decide to care for another dog, remember that he is a different pet and has a distinct character all his own. If you had a purebred dog, consider choosing a different breed to avoid being reminded too much of your previous pet. However, when making a choice, it is not a good idea to stray too far from the previous breed. If you were happy with a toy breed, it is not a good idea to choose a breed with radically different needs, such as a rottweiler.

Memories of your dog can help you come to terms with his departure. With time, you'll be able to think of him fondly without feelings of sadness.

Resources

Reading

The following books will provide information that complements the material found in *Young at Heart*.

Alderton, D. *Fat Dog Thin*, Hamlyn, London, 2007.
Flaim, D. *The Holistic Dog Book: Canine Care for the 21st Century*, Howell Book House, New York, 2003.
Fogle, B. *Caring for Your Dog*, Dorling Kindersley, London, 2002.
Fox, M. W. *The Healing Touch for Dogs: The Proven Massage Program for Dogs*, Newmarket Press, New York, 2004.
Hourdebaigt, J. P. *Canine Massage: A Complete Reference Manual*, Dogwise Publishing, Wenatchee, Washington, 2003.
Kamen, D. R. *The Well-adjusted Dog: Canine Chiropractic Methods You Can Do*, Brookline, Cambridge, Massachusetts, 1996.
Schwartz, C. *Four Paws Five Directions: A Guide to Chinese Medicine for Cats and Dogs*, Newmarket Press, New York, 2004.
Snow, A. *The Well-connected Dog: A Guide to Canine Acupressure*, Tallgrass Publishers, Larkspur, Colorado, 1999.

Web Resources

Listed below are various organizations related to senior dogs and their care, as well as some general information about dogs. Also included are some sites that specialize in products for dogs. Their inclusion does not imply endorsement. This list is not inclusive, and you may find other sources on the Internet. If you don't have access to a computer at home, you can visit a local library to use one.

In the United States

American Kennel Club

This organization provides a website filled with information about dog breeds and breeders.
www.akc.org

Ani-Med

Sponsored by the ASPCA, a resource of pet care information, providing medical, nutritional, and behavioral needs for keeping your dog (or other pet) healthier and happier.
www.ani-med.org

Association for Pet Loss and Bereavement

A compassionate nonprofit organization runs this website, which is dedicated to helping people during periods of bereavement.
www.aplb.org

CDSindogs.com

This website helps owners of dogs with cognitive dysfunction syndrome (CDS).
www.cdsindogs.com

DogAge

This website provides general information about senior dog care, including preventive health care, infections and diseases, dietary information, and weight control.
www.dogage.com/care

Dog Owner's Guide

An online magazine that provides a wealth of information on dog-related matters, from adopting a puppy or senior dog, breed profiles, and dogs at work and play to food and nutrition, manners and training, and veterinary information.
www.canismajor.com/dog/

Fancy Paws

Supplier of dog products, including heated dog beds, ramps, and feeders.
www.fancypaws.com

HandicappedPets.com

Provides products, services, and support for elderly, disabled, and handicapped pets. Products available include carts, special-needs beds, protective boots, items for safe travel, and natural supplements.
www.HandicappedPets.com

Just4Pooches

Supplier of dog equipment and accessories, including raised bowls, portable bowls, dog beds, ramps, and natural remedies.
www.just4pooches.com

K-9 Cart Company East

Supplier of carts designed to help immobile dogs become mobile. They also provide diapers and other hygienic products for mobility impaired dogs.
www.mri.jhmi.edu/~dara/index.php

The Natural Canine

Supplier of natural and homeopathic remedies.
www.naturalcanine.com

My Pet Pages

This web page offers a listing of websites for those who are grieving the loss of a pet.
www.mypetpages.net/petresources/category.php?id=35

PetAlive.com

Supplier of natural herbal remedies for dogs.
www.nativeremedies.com/petalive

The PetCenter.com

An Internet animal hospital website with information on dog care, written by vets and photographed in animal hospitals with the goal of providing accurate and easily understood pet health care information.
www.thePetCenter.com

The Senior Dog House and Rescue

A website dedicated to rescuing, adopting, and living with senior dogs.
www.arescuemom.org

The Senior Dogs Project

A website dedicated to finding homes for senior dogs. It provides a broad listing of agencies that help to rehome senior dogs and will find a dog to adopt or seek help in placing a dog through these agencies. It also provides heartwarming success stories about adoptions and tips on how to care for senior dogs.
www.srdogs.com

Senior Pet Products.com

Supplier of dog products, including raised bowls, dog beds, ramps, and natural remedies. Also offers discussion boards and a library of useful information on dog health.
www.seniorpetproducts.com

ValleyVet.com

Supplier of dog equipment and accessories, including beds, toys, paw protectors, harnesses, and portable water bowls.
www.valleyvet.com/ct_pet.html

Veterinary Information for Dog Owners

This website is a valuable resource for dog owners seeking information on veterinary medicine. However, the site is not intended to replace the advice of your veterinarian.
www.vetinfo4dogs.com/dogindex.html

In Canada

Adopt an Animal—Canada

Volunteers in Vancouver, Edmonton, Toronto, and Montreal arrange for dogs and other animals to be adopted by suitable owners throughout Canada.
www.adoptananimal.ca

Canada's Guide to Dogs

A website providing in-depth information on dog breeds and breeders, listings and details on shelters and rescue organizations, and material on health, nutrition, and training your dog.
www.canadasguidetodogs.com/index.htm

Canadian Kennel Club

A nonprofit, national organization focused on the promotion and advancement of purebred dogs.
www.ckc.ca

Index

Picture Credits and Acknowledgments

Picture Credits

Ardea: John Daniels 51, 121, 129; Jean Paul Ferrero 10-11, 143; Michel Labat 145; Johan de Meester 105, 115.

Ian Armitage/© Toucan Books 85, 87, 117, 119.

Elizabeth Barrington 152.

Barry Blitz 45.

Corbis: Ami Chappell 109; Dann Tardif 17.

Andy Crawford/© Toucan Books 67.

Empics: Deutsche Press Agent 114; Martin Rickett 112, 139.

Leah Germann 139.

www.HandicappedPets.com 70, 73, 116b.

Kaspurgold Kennels 12r.

Charlotte Lowndes /© Toucan Books 14, 20, 48, 54, 84, 103, 123, 134.

Dean McLachlan/© Toucan Books 6-7, 9, 13, 18, 22-23, 25, 27, 29, 30-31, 33, 34, 35-37, 42, 44, 47, 53, 55-58, 60-62, 64, 68-69, 71, 74-80, 83, 94-95, 97, 107T, 111, 125, 127, 130, 133, 137, 146-149, 151l, 151r, 152-153.

NHPA: Susanne Danegger 88-89; Ernie Janes 38.

Rex Features: Alban Donohoe(ADO) 107b.

Science Photo Library: Mauro Fermariello 104, Robert Holmgren, Peter Arnold Inc 116t.

Shutterstock.com: Antonela 113; Tim Elliott 82; Leah Groisberg 93; Judy Ben Joud 131; Theresa Martinez 140; Natzbaer 132M; Knud Nielsen 86; Steven Pepple 40-41; Petr 135; Tina Rencell 15; Rachel Sellers 12m; Magdalena Sobczk 2-3; Eline Spek 59; Joanne Stemberger 12L; April Turner 43.

The DogMobile Company: www.dogmobile-online.com 72.

Graham White: 90, 98, 100, 102, 108, 110, 118, 124, 126, 128.

Roy Williams: 8, 61, 65.

Acknowledgments

Thanks to the following owners who kindly allowed their dogs to be in our book:

Elizabeth Barrington (Mandy), Vicky Beard (Mollie and Sally), Pat Brewster (Ellie), Richard Burlinson (Jem and Jade), David Cole (Rosy), Gail Colthurst (Jarvis), Sarah Dewfall (Teddy and Dotty), John Dugay (B. B. and Twist), Pauline Edwards and Ken Bye (Sally), Susan Hocking and the Kaspurgold dogs, Jane Holmes (Hydee), Derek Jay and Claire Hambley (Cha-chi, Daisy, Oscar, Jamil), Ellie Lewis (Milo), Kathy Longhurst (Bentley), Brian and Peggy Marchant (Billy), Jane Marshall (Dan), Peter and Ann Moffit (Billie), Jackie Portingale (Rudy), Doug and Sue Richardson (Ben, Sparky, Tammy, and Ali), Clare Scott (Peebles and Boss), Susan Slade (Izzie), Ginny Snape (Margot), Ian Stuart and Kathryn Nicholls (Zog), Mary Summerfield (Willa), John Sunter (Billie), Sandra Thexton (Daisy May and Flora), Marian Wild (Rowan), Abbie Yeeles and (Reuben and Harry).

Thanks to: Ian Armitage, Mary Frances Budzik, Sarah Bebbington, Hannah Bowen, and Jackie Mobsby.

With special thanks to Dean McLachlan for his terrific photos and to his dog Sammy, and to everyone at Handicapped Pets.